THE

MASSACRE

AT SAND CREEK

AMERICAN INDIAN LITERATURE
AND CRITICAL STUDIES SERIES

Gerald Vizenor and Louis Owens, General Editors

THE

MASSACRE

AT SAND CREEK

NARRATIVE VOICES

BY

BRUCE CUTLER

UNIVERSITY OF OKLAHOMA PRESS

NORMAN AND LONDON

Portions of this work have appeared previously,
sometimes in slightly different form, in the following publications:
Juniper Press, LaCrosse, WI, Juniper Book #55:
"The Letters of Silas Soule"; *Kansas Quarterly*: "The Attack,"
"The Old Gentleman on the Train"; *The Spoon River Quarterly*: "A Burial."
"The Attack" won a *Kansas Quarterly* First Award for Poetry.

The characters depicted in this narrative bear a strong resemblance to their historical namesakes. While many of their actions and statements are carefully reported, their motivations can only be a matter of conjecture. I have taken liberties in this area on their behalf as have the many historians and commentators whose work has stimulated me over the last three decades.

My thanks to the National Endowment for the Arts
and the Bush Foundation for the fellowships
that made the writing of this book possible.

This book is published with the generous assistance of
Edith Gaylord Harper.

LIBRARY OF CONGRESS CATALOGING-IN-PUBLICATION DATA
Cutler, Bruce, 1930–
   The massacre at Sand Creek / by Bruce Cutler.
       p.   cm. — (American Indian literature and critical studies
   series ; v. 16)
   ISBN 0-8061-2673-6
   1. Indians of North America—Colorado—Poetry.   2. Sand Creek
Massacre, Colo., 1864—Poetry.   3. Cheyenne Indians—Wars, 1864—
Poetry.   I. Title.   II. Series.
PS3553.U8M38   1995
811'.54—dc20
                                                              94-31306
                                                                  CIP

Text design: Christine Taylor
Composition: Wilsted & Taylor Publishing Services

The Massacre at Sand Creek is Volume 16
in the American Indian Literature and Critical Studies Series.

The paper in this book meets the guidelines for permanence and durability
of the Committee on Production Guidelines for Book Longevity
of the Council on Library Resources. ♾

1 2 3 4 5 6 7 8 9 10

CONTENTS

Preface   *vii*

1

The Wolves of Heaven, August 14, 1911   *5*

The Letters of Silas Soule,
November 12, 1861–November 15, 1862   *17*

The Wolves of Heaven, Morning, August 15, 1911   *31*

The Letters of Silas Soule, April 1, 1863   *41*

2

The Wolves of Heaven, Afternoon, August 15, 1911   *53*

The Letters of Silas Soule,
October 7, 1863–August 29, 1864   *65*

The Wolves of Heaven, Morning, August 16, 1911   *75*

The Letters of Silas Soule, October 9, 1864   *85*

3

The Attack, November 29, 1864   *93*

The Letters of Silas Soule,
February 12, 1865–April 15, 1865   *113*

The Wolves of Heaven, Afternoon, August 16, 1911   *121*

4

Clipping from the *Rocky Mountain News*,
April 27, 1865   *129*

An Interview with Colonel John Milton Chivington,
November 30, 1868   *133*

The Wolves of Heaven, Morning, August 17, 1911   *147*

An Interview with Colonel John Milton Chivington,
Continued, November 31, 1868   *157*

The Wolves of Heaven, Afternoon, August 17, 1911   *175*

5

The Wolves of Heaven, August 18, 1911   *193*

The Old Gentleman on the Train, June 8, 1871   *211*

The Wolves of Heaven, August 19, 1911   *235*

PREFACE

On November 29, 1864, in the last weeks of the Civil War, a force of territorial militia under the command of a politically ambitious former Methodist minister, Col. John Milton Chivington, attacked a sleeping camp of Cheyennes along Sand Creek in the southeast part of the Colorado Territory. John Evans, the governor of the territory, had previously authorized the organization of this militia for defense against a Confederate invasion, but the invasion never came. However, in the interim, there had been several bloody clashes between Cheyennes and newly arrived white settlers.

Evans had advocated a policy of separating hostile and friendly tribal units and of protecting the latter in certain specified enclaves. Now, fears generated by the clashes caused him to decide that most of the Plains Indian tribes should be pursued as enemies of the country. He issued a proclamation to this effect without bothering to inform the tribes of his decision, and he dramatized the situation by appearing armed in public, saying that it was the duty of every man to defend himself at all times.

Behind Evans and his policies loomed the figure of his

friend, Chivington. Chivington was a candidate for Congress, thirsting to regain the military glory he had won at a battle against Confederate forces earlier in the war. He proclaimed that Indians would kill women and children, he damned any man in sympathy with Indians, and he now believed it right and honorable to use any means under God's heaven to kill them. His militia were "Hundred Daysers," so-called for the short period of their enlistment. Many of them were unemployed miners and drifters. They saw an attack on Indians, any Indians, as a popular move in a war they knew would soon end.

Black Kettle was a peace chief of the Cheyennes. He believed his camp at Sand Creek was a safe enclave, and he had gathered around him a group of nonbelligerents. It was against them that Chivington launched a surprise attack at dawn; what ensued was genocide. Hundreds of Cheyennes and Arapahoes were massacred, two-thirds of whom were women and children. John Smith, a well-known mountain man and trapper who was visiting the camp at the time of the raid, had his life spared, but his half-Cheyenne son was killed. Smith was forced to watch as the body was dragged around the camp behind the horses of Chivington's men.

Shortly before the attack, while on his way to Sand Creek at the head of his militia, Chivington happened to pass by Fort Lyon and made an unexpected request for additional troops of the First Colorado Regiment stationed there. These regular troops had actually been charged with keeping order between Indians and whites, and they had recently arranged for a truce with the Plains tribes. After lengthy discussion, and vigorous dissent by some of the First Colorado officers, Chivington obtained agreement from the fort command for additional troops. Several officers continued to feel that the projected raid would be "murder, pure and simple." One of them was Captain Silas Soule, a veteran of the border warfare between abolitionists and proslavery forces in Kansas in the years prior to the Civil War. At the moment of the attack, when Soule realized the full impact of Chivington's purpose, he refused to order his men to fire. From that moment, Soule earned Chivington's enmity.

Controversy over Sand Creek arose quickly. Many saw that Chivington's assault had compromised the good-faith efforts of the regular army to maintain order with the Cheyennes and other Plains tribes. The controversy generated several congressional inquiries. Chivington maintained the rightness of his conduct. Soule was the first to testify against him, and his testimony, along with that of others, remained firm. Each of the inquiries found that Chivington had ordered an unprovoked assault, but in the end, no punishment could be meted out to him because it was discovered that his commission had actually expired before he had undertaken the raid. In this climate of legal and administrative chaos, the Civil War ended. Within a few days came the assassination of President Lincoln, and a few days after that, Soule himself became the target of an assassin and was shot and killed.

The massacre at Sand Creek, like the My Lai massacre in our time, was an atrocity committed during a period of escalating hostilities between indigenous peoples and their European invaders. Violence worsened in the aftermath of Sand Creek, and it became more and more common among white Americans to believe that their government's Indian policy should reflect a ruthlessness based on the assumption that Indians not only would, but must, disappear altogether. Politicians felt increasingly free to assert that Indians "were not an improvable breed." The destiny of American Indians in such a climate of opinion inexorably turned toward racial extermination.

In the years since, the Cheyennes' struggle to maintain themselves, their language, their religion, and their identity as a people has been extremely difficult. Often it has been a losing struggle. But during our century, there has developed a tidal wave of demand for the rights of subject peoples that has swept the continents of the world, including our own, stirring change. What was a minority view of the worth, dignity, and rights of American Indians at the time of Silas Soule and Black Kettle has become more representative of a majority view today.

It is a Cheyenne view of the world that is reflected in the Massaum sections of this narrative. The Massaum has been one of the ancient threads that has held the Cheyenne people together. As you read about Ekomina, Frank Little Wolf, and the Massaum ceremony itself, you will encounter short groups of lines on a page, sometimes even one-line pages. Take them as suggestions of the enduring differences between the Cheyenne language and our own. The world of

Ekomina and Frank Little Wolf both cries out for and asserts the authenticity of its vision through my attempt to render the Cheyenne language.

I am indebted to many people who have been helpful to me since that day in 1959 when I decided to start work on this project, not least to the anthropologist Karl Schlesier, whose work in reconstructing the content of the Massaum ceremony, which had its last known re-enactment in Montana in August of 1911, is reflected here in the title of the Massaum sections. And my special thanks to James Lee Burke, who believed in this book.

BRUCE CUTLER

THE

MASSACRE

AT SAND CREEK

1

THE WOLVES OF HEAVEN

Northern Cheyenne Reservation, Montana
August 14, 1911

*What really belongs to anybody,
except what they have already
lived? What has anybody
to live for, except what they
are not yet living?*

CESARE PAVESE

▼

They're camped in short-grass country, but it isn't theirs.
In a place that they've been given, if given is what
you can't say "no" to.

               A place that they would ride through
to get to another place, if the whites would let them.
To a place where sky and earth connect, where the spirit
world can bless and guide the living. Where all
can know the dead when living, and the living when they're
   dead.
In peace.

Instead, they dig. The man and woman take
turns, under a stone-colored sky. Not a tree,
not a thing that moves except for the glint
of the mattock, rising, falling.

        There's a bundle at their feet.
It's wrapped in grasses and a bolt of flannel, tied
with thongs. It has come to her from Oklahoma
from a cousin of a cousin who came on the thing it holds.
In a white man's store of hand-me-downs. The cousin
had known at once, wedged as it was in a corner
in back of shoes and purses where it lived on, forgotten.
It was tanned and supple and bordered with a casing
stitched in red, with a French silk drawstring run
inside to close it. No need for a second look,
she'd known.

        How could the white man know? What he felt
he let pass through his heart. It left him without memory,
in ignorance that spared him from the gall of shame.

She thinks: you can ask of Owl "Who are the most
on earth, the living or the dead?" and Owl will say
"The dead!" And there you are, truth is told
on you, say as you will "Since when is it
success for anyone to die?"
                                    For saying that
you betray a heart that doubts the wonder of this world.
This place where fear should never light its fire.
This place of transformations. Deathlessness. Miracle.

.

So she asks nothing. This thing that is now a bauble
has passed from hand to hand, relative to relative,
has made its way as a stray dog would across
the plains, until it found her. Cradled by hands,
by palms, by fingers, it took on life, came out
of its past like a ghost, branded with the name of the man
who once had worked it into shape, "Squiers, S. Crk.,
1864."
      And it was truly a child
of its maker. So cunning, so aweless it could stay on a shelf
or in back of a drawer for years unless you took it
carefully in hand, felt its surface, traced
its contours down to the hard unyielding areola
and nipple at the bottom. Then you would have known.

·

The cousins, they had known. And now the woman
has it, this piece, this bit of pelt that never
was the pouch it posed as, that never served
a purpose other than to fit a message to your hand,
terrible phylactery of the faith that holds an Indian
less than a living soul.
                Tit-bag, soldiers
called it. It has come along with wizened fingers,
scalplocks, scrotums stretched into humidors,
the file of body parts that slipped away
in pockets, kit-bags, trunks, leaving the plains
for courthouse squares, banquet halls, museums.

And then into the long dark night of dresser drawers,
attic trunks. Waiting. Continuing to be.
Biding the time until their time would come again.

Today, she's vowed she'll give it burial. She,
the woman, Ekomina, granddaughter of Crow Woman that died
in the white man's trap at Sandy Creek. She,
at work with her husband, Frank Little Wolf. The two of them,
pledgers for the Massaum. But first they must dig a narrow
house for the thousandth part of one of them, their people,
Tsistsistas.

·

"Deep enough." Frank Little Wolf lays down
his tools. He spits on his hands, then hers.
They lay
the bundle in the little deep-earth lodge, filling it
back up along with prayers and pledges and scantlings
of tobacco. She prays that every bone and every
piece of skin and every hair of all
their people will have a narrow house like this some day.

For the story is there wasn't even half of Crow Woman
left to bury when they'd found her after Sandy Creek.
Story that was repeated, day after week after year
as the whites had come at them, pushed them onto
    reservations.

They'd broken out, tried to trek to Canada,
but troops had forced them back.

                          A flock of wild
geese, that straggled from marsh to river, starting
up, beaten down, starting up again.
Their broken bodies blanketing the landscape.

•

Here is the little grave. The copper-colored
clods, pressed down and banked. Less than a body-
length, only a few spans wide, it seems
just the slightest catch of breath in the gritty
thorax of plains and sky.
                               Spirit-wind, breath
sent out from the spirit world, bring blessing to this place
and to this people—she feels the words pass through
her soul, enter the air like fledgling eagles.
Sharp-eyed. Craving. Catch-as-catch-can.

.

Prayers, to a stone-colored sky.

THE LETTERS OF SILAS SOULE

November 12, 1861–November 15, 1862

There is properly no history;
only biography.

R. W. EMERSON

▼

Raton, New Mexico Territory
November 12, 1861

Dearest Mother,

You see, I made it pat!
Major Kit Carson sends you greetings and grateful
thanks for festive board, back when Father
was still alive. He asks me do I think
if I could rescue one more Doctor Doy
from the Rebs, or Mexicans, or Injuns? How's that
for my reputation coming out ahead
of me! And so much the better—I'm finally out
of Kansas and on the Taos Trail. In short,
today I'm made lieutenant in Kit's own company!
Since the gold rush up in Colorado,
ores are on everybody's mind out here,
the mountains gleam with veins of quartz. But the light
mellows them with lavenders and blues
and purples, plus something you'd say is like the sea,

that deep-water green off the coast of our beloved
Maine. Though here, the green's most likely malachite.
I guess your boy won't get rich soon—he'll have
to dog for grub, instead of dig for gold!
Did Annie buy a one-way ticket back
to Maine? Wouldn't you know that Sis would funk
at chills and fever and a hundred-fourteen in the shade.
But that's the scratch that cures the Kansas itch.
Give her my love. And a brotherly devoir
to W. L. G., if he's still alive and on
the Union side.

Your devoted,
Si

November 28, 1861
To: Mr. Walter Whitman, c/o Thayer,
    Eldridge, Hinton, etc.

Dear Walt,

When you think you've seen all the world and you want
to get up another book, first come out
second-class as far as Kansas. Then head
on down the Taos Trail. But I don't suppose
you'd want to leave your palmy life at Pfaff's
Cafe and literary loafing just to watch
the buzzards circling overhead and hear them bidding
for your brains. Gravely speaking, that's how it is here—
now for the lighter side! I haven't told
my mother but I spent the summer of '60 looking
for Golconda, up in Colorado. What I found
was Geneva Gulch. The eve of my arrival
we went bare-knuckles and one of the boys had his eye
displaced about a half a knuckle out-of-socket,
whereupon we rechristened it as Gouge-Eye Gulch.
It's one rough spot to slosh a placer pan
or feed a rackety quartz mill, just for grub.
Talk about fatigue! After a month
high in the Rockies where nothing boils but tempers
anything in this Army seems a snap! One day
at dusk, someone said he wounded an elk
that plunged into a gorge and got away. We rode,

then walked, then stalked the blood-spoor up a ridge,
then struck a chasm where the moon could cast no light
and smack, a heavy growl shook the ground. Two balls
of fiery eyes, our rifles emptied at the mark,
and instead of a stately elk we brought a nine-foot
cougar down. His arms were big as millposts!
Here I am in a troop of volunteers
who can't tell elk from cougar—wait till the war
breaks out in earnest, then even French-Canadians
will be running for their lives! You see when you come out
how well us folks will treat you? In any case
I have a lot to say about you, wherever
I go, and no, I don't think people realize
how long this war may last. They say not long,
our Union with more than twenty million souls
against a piddling five of Rebs, but I'm
not fooled. My little rescue party, that sprung
old Doctor Doy from the Saint Joe jail, ran
into postmasters, detectives, agents of the Treasury
Department, U.S. attorneys, field commanders
and a web of touts and toughs all deep inside
the borders of a "loyal" state, who sink or swim
would have it that the rule of slavery will prevail.
You know all this from when I saw you back
in Gotham, yet there's more to tell. Then, I only
mentioned weeks I spent to try and spring
John Brown from his cell at Harper's Ferry—but it takes
a better nib than the one surviving in this Army

pen for that, so I'll wait to tell you next time.
Yes, send your book to me. Us troopers guard
the mails and almost everything gets through
except for apple butter and toilet soap
that have a way of getting sidetracked in Missouri.
Your *Leaves of Grass* will make it here for sure!

As ever,
        Si

        P.S. Your poems will help
to save this Territory from the plague
of verse in vogue. Beautiful Dutch, it's called.
Here's one:

        Cot tam dat shnaik vot pites mine shon,
        He's all over plack, mit fite shpots on;
        He laish in ter grass, and he fistle mit him tail.
        Cot tam dat Cot tam shnaik to Hail.

                                No more.
Weep, for the Muse is spent—till payday.

                        S.

Denver, Colorado Territory
November 15, 1862

Dear Sis,

  Mom writes you're back in Maine, working—
typesetter, proofreader, like-it-or-not amender
of all that cometh out of the mouth and onto
the page in Bangor. Selah! Are all those Baptists
ready for some tales of barracks life?
No need to answer. I'll write, you print what's fit.
Herewith the chronicle of the tribes of U.S. Cavalry
and the wanderings of your lost brother, Si. Six words:
The West is saved, Colorado ours!
And now, for how it happened. The last you heard
of me was from New Mexico. I'd just
been made lieutenant by Kit Carson. But soon
I found the Scouts don't mix it up the way
I'd fancied. I recalled your favorite bard, "Whither
shall I betake me—where subsist?" only I
would have it "—where to fight?" The governor here
in Colorado settled me by ordering up
a regiment of volunteers last Christmas,
the Colorado First. They call it infantry
but lots of us showed up on horseback, many
out of Carson's Scouts. They made me first
lieutenant, Company K, my first assignment
keeping order in the ranks. Christmas '61

brought out the Cossack urge to forage through the
    alleyways
of Denver City, picking hen-roost locks and lifting
forty-gallon barrels (of vinegar, alas!).
At a knothole, a pistol would appear, at a trap-hole
piggies disappeared. And how our cooks did cook!
You see—no pay, no money in the company for months,
and lo! the eighth of deadly sins—Jayhawking!
The good governor and his minion Methodists
confined our Regiment to barracks, with one
result—we only came to barracks for our meals!
So much for keeping order, hot water through a sieve.
But drill we did, all through the winter, and so clear
the air you could see the glaciers inching
down the Front Range of the Rockies. By March we were a
    mostly
sober Regiment, ready to campaign. Though once
in a while we'd have to strip a company of their arms
and put them under arrest for mutiny. They wanted
to be paid, and fight the Rebs, in equal measure!
At last, Fort Leavenworth sent word for us to join
with General Canby in New Mexico,
recapture Albuquerque and Santa Fe
from General Sibley's Texans. Our highest in command
run true to type—they're Masons, setters of cornerstones,
elders and deacons and boon companions of the governor,
in short, not worth one impious expletive
of a peripatetic repairer of damaged tin!

But our major proved exception to the rule.
John Chivington by name, Chiv for short—
he's hardly short at six foot four, two hundred
sixty pounds, barrel chest, and neck
of a mature male bovine (to your Baptists)! Once a
    preacher,
he flat refused a praying commission for the fighting
one—to all our satisfactions, as you'll see.
We rode along the Front Range down to Pueblo,
then up across the Raton Pass through freshets
of melting winter snows. At Trinidad
we met the courier from Fort Union. The Rebs were on
the march along the Rio Grand again,
the Fort was sure to fall! The major drew us
up in line and asked if we would make
forced march that night. We just had done enough
day's march to turn old Natty Bumppo bottle-green
with envy, but off we slogged again, riding
the wagons when our strength gave out. We did
sixty-four miles in four-and-twenty
hours, consecutive, and finally found the Rebs
strung out across Apache Canyon. Old Chiv
arranged our battle lines, the enemy was engaged
and when we charged it was one of those things I dreamed
to see when I was a boy—a mountain of a man
on a coal-black stallion, with ninety-nine of us
behind him, sabers drawn, charging through
their ranks, our pistols flashing, slashing, drubbing,

sabering, slaughtering. Quoth Chiv, "I know of nothing
else to do but fight!" The Rebs had never
seen our like, and when sundown came, they threw
down their arms and ran for the hills. Then we
had everything to do. We took one Rebel prisoner
for every one of us upon that field.
Plus care for the wounded. Bury the dead. And try
to save some strength, for more was sure to come.
But how their officers argued! You'd think they'd won
the battle and the war instead of bumbling into capture.
As if states rights and slavery were a Bible tract
to hallelujah in our ears. At the end, I cut
contention short with my favorite phrase from childhood—
"You may have the argument, but by God, I know
I'm right!" You remember how it does the trick.
Next morning it was march again, to Glorieta Pass,
two miles from where we'd fought them. It was their
    reserves—
munitions and supplies and a caravan of wagons
mules and horses snaking up the valley
out of a giant egg of dust. This time
we took them from the mountainsides, surprised
the guards, spiked their supplies, ran their wagons
all together, put them to the torch.
General Sibley sent his flag of truce
begging leave to tend his wounded. In fact,
he used the truce as cover for retreat. He even
left his dead for us to bury. So much

for Southern chivalry! But then, the hardest thing
of all was what came last, first to corral
then bayonet 1100 mules and horses
left behind, to leave the Rebs without
a way to hold New Mexico or Colorado
or anything west of Texas or north of the Rio
Grand. It was a bath of blood and screaming
animals, but we did it, Sis. And no one now
can call us bloodless—we're Colorado's First!
So we're back in Denver, another Christmas
almost here, and Governor Evans says
we'll all be formally transferred to cavalry.
Our major soon will be a colonel. Who knows—
I'll soon be pushing silver bars. Captain
Soule—wouldn't that just shoot the works? What would
our little brother think? Whoever hears
from him—do you? It seems six centuries ago,
(but six years only) that our teeth were chattering like
    spoons
in a minstrel band inside our cabin down
on Coal Creek, Kansas Territory. You hated it, it ruined
Father's health, the slavery issue staggered
on, one decade to the next. Kansas—the place
where almost nothing can come out (except the sun),
where almost everything runs out (I mean
your brains, your hope, your chips) (Baptists read that
soul, and silver lining, and distinctive tokens
of contingency)! I miss us. I haven't got a soul

to tease, no one quotes a line of poetry
or brightens up my day with wholly useless
facts. I know if you came here you'd send your heart
in care of General Delivery, you'd find a way to nurse
the wounded, console the living, rescind our judgment
on those mules—after a week or so
you'd make this wicked Denver City a Jerusalem!
We'd be driving big bright bays, and listening to the doves
and swallows at the eaves. Dreaming of youth and
    freedom,
boundless as the sunshine is for all.

Your,

Si

THE WOLVES OF HEAVEN

Northern Cheyenne Reservation, Montana
Morning, August 15, 1911

*The world is not so much a noun
as an adjective.*

GASTON BACHELARD

▼

The woman and the man—Ekomina, Frank Little Wolf—
they've left the burial behind, they're riding slowly
down to a river, to a sacred place, to the trees
along the banks. To a camp, the gathering of the people.

She can see the lodge poles in the distance, smell
the cooking fires. She hears dogs, yapping.

Beyond those sounds she hears a great heart beating.
The presence of something other.
                              Cold heart, beating.

．

The two of them are pledgers for the Massaum.
His are the hands that will dig a lodge where the sacred
tree will rise.
                    Hers are the hands that will raise
the trunk of that tree with lodge poles.
                                        No man will touch
    it,
no other hand will touch it.
                        And the tree will grow!

.

"We are here!" they call as they arrive, and then again
"We are here!" at the door of every lodge in camp.

Now they're ready. They're together with the people, in a
  land
that isn't theirs. Ready for the oldest thing
they know. The oldest thing the world's alive to.

Their pledge for the world to be reborn.
                                    The Massaum.

·

The people gather round. Now Ekomina can begin
to say her Story:

> *They were camped in tall-grass country.*
> *But it wasn't theirs. They were confused. Game went into*
>   *hiding.*
> *Nothing to eat. Nothing.*

> *It was a time to save*
> *the people. All of them together. Time to send out*
> *scouts. To straighten out the way. To bring*
> *good news.*

> *So two go out, and they find their way.*
> *Day after day they go, until for all*
> *fatigue, and footsore, they've found the way to the den*
> *of death.*

．

*Then they see The Mountain, blue
in the blue of sky. A lake lies shining at its base.
Better to die on the mountain, both of them.*

*They make a last half-day, and come to the water.
That's when the water breaks and a great horned serpent
wreathes around the younger one. Coil
upon coil it comes, and he cries out in the power that holds
   him.
The serpent takes him under.*

·

*The other, the elder,
is a shaman and a healer. A man who knows just how
to pray, how to be heard in the spirit world.
Keep on, is the message in his blood. So he keeps on going.*

*A sudden rush of wolfskin stops him. It's a man
covered in a Red Wolf skin who dodges him, strikes
the water, tears the water open, takes
the serpent by the nape and cuts its throat.*

·

The man then turns to the elder. "Climb," he says,
"climb the mountain, find the standing rock!
That rock will be a door. Put your shoulder to the rock
and make it move, and then you'll see a woman
old as the mountain. Tell her this. Tell her
I the grandfather killed the serpent, the cunning
serpent I've been hunting all my life!"

THE LETTERS OF SILAS SOULE

April 1, 1863

*Great historical transformations
are always bought dearly,
often after you thought you
got them at a bargain price.*

JAKOB BURCKHARDT

Messrs. Thayer, Eldridge, Hinton, etc.
Boston, Massachusetts

Gentlemen,

Mr. Walter Whitman lays it pretty
thick if he thinks my little stories of escape
might touch a reader's finer sensibilities.
At this late hour in the War of the Rebellion
they may be more for the archives than beating drums.
It all commenced nine years ago, in a time
almost inconceivable to me now. My father
was Amasa Soule. He brought our family out
to Kansas Territory south of Lawrence
with Company Five, Emigrant Aid. Coal Creek
was our claim, all knew that we were abolitionists,
my younger brother went by the name of William
Lloyd Garrison Soule. Proof enough, we said,
that we were a line of true down-Easters! But
more a squiggle than a line, as it turned out.
Malignant powers hemmed us in, Missouri
and the U.S. Marshal played the devil with our enterprise,
and it wasn't long before we saw Fort Scott
and Franklin Pierce as evil twins, two peas
in a pod in the arbor of calamity. Our freedom road

for slaves was spied on constantly by a mongrel league
of thugs, Treasury detectives, postmasters, and deserters
bent on bounty hunting. On our side, the totally
unqualified rallied to the cause, I mean enthusiasts
esteemed for want of any caution and experience,
not to mention judgment. They came out West
from Boston, trim on their English saddles, eager
to act as troupers in a spectacle called Kansas.
Doctor Doy was a black Republican. But when he thought
to intervene in anything, be it erysipelas
or slavery, he gave new meanings to his sobriquet,
    Sawbones.
It was Reverend Ephraim Nute who gave him leave
to escort up a dozen contrabands with families
and not a single scout, no rear guard,
nothing. Of course the mongrel league surprised him,
seized the fugitives, the women, children, wagons,
everything, turning them back toward Missouri
and slavery once again. So Doy was taken.
Missouri tried him, Kansas defended him, the jury
finally did convict him. He got five years
on the first of twelve indictments. In time, the total
might have come to sixty years, with much abuse
and villainy, and certain death. We gave up hope
of all appeals. We saw we'd have to take him
from his jail. Between us Coal Creek boys was $30
cash, 3 sporting rifles, a few revolvers,
knives, a slung-shot cast in lead. Not one

Sharps rifle could we use, these being the giveaway
for abolitionists. We came to see that guile
would have to do what force could not. It was then
my youthful years in a whiting factory came
to hand, the brogue of Irish workers gripped
my tongue, the Pat-and-Mike jokes frolicked out
along with a taste for whiskey and a tenor's croon.
That was the birth of Doyle O'Boyle, the rebaptized
Silas Soule. And he was vital to the plan.
Do you know the one about the impish boy
and the Baptist preacher? It seems this preacher railed
for years against the fleshpots, and in time, he
    bushwhacked
most of what Old Scratch laid claim to. Hardly
a dram or a dance or a friendly faro game
survived his slaughter of the venial. An April Sunday
capped the climax, a great baptizing at the riverbank,
the preacher led his lambs, the water glistened
grandly in the sun. But one rogue boy there was
who liked a friendly round at cards. He hallelujahed
right along with everyone, but when the preacher
raised his arms and closed his eyes, he slipped
a deck inside the sunless folds of that man's
gown. Then step by step as Preacher Blight
submerged, a spade-and-club armada sailed
out of his holy folds and the waves
did blush with forbidden hearts and diamonds! At last,
there was absolutely nothing he could say.

Well, that was the way I came to town, with gab
and gullery for all. I made the others come
as Pike's Peak boys, impatient to set out, chafing
to buy a team and wagon. O'Boyle
would want to sell them one, and so we all
would move together through the streets,
saloon after saloon. I also had to find
the jailer, prick his boredom with a tale or two,
then say I bore a word from Doy's dear wife.
He was a decent sort. He told me to deliver it.
"He who tempers the winds to a chit of a lamb
will not forget His child, who suffers for the kindness
done unfortunates," I brogued, convincingly.
The jailer wiped a tear. The doctor stood
agape. My eye surveyed the cell. I kept
on talking, lest the doctor gave it all away.
Then I passed a message in a ball of twine,
"Tonight—at twelve o'clock." Later on we found
we had the luck, the Duke of Dimmley Players
were putting on *The Orphan's Tragedy*
that night to benefit the Scottish Masons.
The sober and the literate thus employed, we seized
on one of us as "horse thief," tied him with the slung-shot
cord, and brought him to the jail. The clouds were thick
and hid the stars, the fog closed in, and you
could almost sink your elbows in that darkness.
Black as the feathers on a crow. Not a street lamp lit,
the windows of the dwellings closed, and those not sober

and the illiterate, asleep. We all held hands,
snaking our way across the square. We banged
on the jailhouse door. A window overhead flew up,
the voice of my friend the keeper rang out clear.
"We have a horse-thief here," I cried. When he opened
up he asked if any had a warrant.
"Citizen arrest!" I said, "this Pike's Peak boy
has tricked me in a sale. He stole my horse, and fled.
We tracked him down and brought him in." And yet
my friend was loath to take him into custody.
He asked him if the charge was true, and was he guilty?
With that, our Pike's Peak boy broke into such
a torrent of abuse that even I was shaken,
ending with, "And I expect to have a trial!"
The jailer took the bait, "I think that you're a thief.
I'll take my chances, and I'll put you in." The doors
opened, and going in we saw a drawing
of a human skeleton. I nudged our Pike's Peak boy.
He balked, "I won't go into such a place!"
"Oh yes you will," the jailer cried, stepping
into the cell where Doy was waiting. Our guns
were leveled, he saw our ruse. The doctor stepped
out free. True to his failing, he'd told the other
prisoners of his imminent release. We had to force
them back at gunpoint in the cell. The jailer now
was much confused. I said he must put out
the light and lock the door and stay confined
till daylight, at peril of his life. He begged me to consider

how we'd compromised him. How could he explain?
They'd think he acted in collusion with our band.
"In the morning you can publish what you will about
this business," was my answer. "When we get home
we'll publish that you never once intended
to assist us." I thanked him for his uniformly kind
demeanor, took him by the hand, and cautioned
him to do as I had said. The moon
was up, *The Orphan's Tragedy* let out, and a brace
of Masons lent us lanterns while we cinched our saddles!
Innocence and cunning, a fatal, lucky pair—
Kansas taught me these, if nothing else.
By February 1860 everything had changed.
The only politician I admired,
James Montgomery, formed a party—Thayer
will recall this all too well, for he was in on it—
Preacher Stewart, Thomas Wentworth Higginson,
me, and eighty others. Our aim was the same,
to free a prisoner, but what a difference in our reach!
John Brown, the man not one of us had trusted
back in Kansas, now enjoyed renown
in places we forever would be nameless. Around him
drew a net of public apprehension.
He simply could not die for the raid at Harper's
Ferry! I packed my traps. Next stop Charles Town
West Virginia where I got myself arrested
drunk, and sobered up on Sunday telling Pat-
and-Mikes and singing jolly songs.

Tell me, why do jailers like me? In a week
I'd wangled what I hadn't dared to hope,
an audience with Brown! Or at least, a talk, if you take
a spare duet of well-armed guards as likely
to redound the camaraderie. What can I say
of that old man that isn't sung by every
schoolboy in the Union? Plenty, is my answer.
Though passing years may throw a haze around
the temple of my memory, that day remains like crystal.
Or better, frozen, as an ice-gray image in my mind.
The old man seemed—so old. Not just because
his sons were martyred, or his ragtag private army
routed. The snow was falling thick, but traveling
the mountains posed no greater hazard, nothing
more impregnable than his own will. "Soule,"
he said—without regard for Doyle O'Boyle,
or the fact I'd penetrated every rampart
just to see him—"Soule, you know as well
as I, our jailer bears no grudges, he's been
much kinder than I think I would have been to him.
You know the state militia keeps its eye
on all of us. But Si, the honor of a thing . . ."
His voice trailed off. When he looked at me again
it was just like staring down a hoary eagle,
"You know as well as I do, only death
on the gallows can bring fulfillment of my mission, the
    rounding
out of all my efforts. No single act

of mine would make my work to free the slaves
effective, more than that." I thought to interpose
objections, that my associates would give their lives
most willingly to set him free again
no matter how the state militia watched
and waited. But I knew that none would move him. He
    said,
"Remember Si—I am worth more to die
than live." As if the whole of thraldom and the crime
of slavery turned upon one single axis,
his own death. And he knew I knew that he was right.
So the last escape was no escape at all.
And Doyle O'Boyle, discharged by an unsuspecting
justice of the peace, absquatulated promptly
to the Quaker State. Lifetime result: one out,
one in. It's not a happy average for a banker,
for a soldier of the line, damn good I'd say. Don't you?
Just remember—you can't save someone who refuses
to be saved! That mark of exclamation should be doubled
when you're detailed to recruiting volunteers,
as I am now. I saw some action at Apache
Canyon, but since, I only write up posters.
"Poor Old Thing! A Bounty to be Paid!
Bull Whackers, Miners, Loyal to Your Country!
Any Man can Come a Pauper and Muster
Out with Money Left to Start a Bank
or Run a Quartz-Mill! You Bet your Life!" and so on.
Thayer should recall a lot of what I say

of this. I haven't had a word from Higginson
in months. The last I knew, he was mail-order writing
master to half the scribbling women in New England.
Now I hear he's colonel to a regiment of coloreds.
Tell him I stake Walt Whitman up against
his belles from Amherst and Poughkeepsie every time!
As for me, my sojourn with the Muse is ended. No more
tippling at the Pierian spring. The local caravansary
serves cocktails: Oporto wine and red rot. Mix.
The net result, a grateful patriot. I'm off.
Fear not. No snakes are lurking in my boots—

                    Yours,
                      Silas Soule
                        P. S.—Yet!

2

THE WOLVES OF HEAVEN

Northern Cheyenne Reservation, Montana
Afternoon, August 15, 1911

*That people could come into the
world in a place they could not
at first even name and never had
known before, and that out of a
nameless and unknown place
they could grow and move
around in it until its name they
knew and called with love, and
called it home, and put roots
there and love others there so
that whenever they left this place
they would sing homesick songs
about it, and write poems of
yearning for it, like a lover—!*

WILLIAM GOYEN

▼

Ekomina has stopped her Story.

Now it's time
to smoke a pipe with the spirit of the tree Frank Little Wolf
must cut down.

It's his turn now to speak:
"Straight young cottonwood: we're here today
to do what we've been told we ought to do
by the two who taught us from the time they learned this
    speaking.
We ask you, be our tree for Massaum. May every
tree and blade of grass and fall of fruit
be hale and thrive forever. And we ask that if
we do not do this duty without mistakes,
forgive us. Forgive our hands. Forgive our hearts."

He fells it. He trims it up, except for seven
branches at the top. Seven, for the seven stars.

                                       And the song
is the woman's song, is the soughing of wind in the boughs
that are singing in the other world.

                                 The two of them drag
the tree to camp. Frank Little Wolf digs five holes.
Four for the points, for the wind-horizons, for the realms
where all find life. And one in the center, the deepest
one, that he must dig before their first day's
work is done.

                  Into it, Ekomina tips the laid-out
tree with lodge poles, up toward heaven, right in the heart
of the Blue-Sky Lodge.

.

Around it, they frame
their lodge. It faces toward The Mountain. Blue Mountain.
It faces toward the lake.

They cover it with skins.
Now the tree of life is standing at the center of their lodge.
It stretches through the smoke hole with its branches
high above. Rustling in wind. Cooling
the skins. Blessing all beneath it with its shade.

.

They name it Wolf Lodge. It's as round as the world
and it doesn't need a door.
                    They scrape up the sod. The
   earth
shines forth.
            They bring white sage. Box-elder wood for a
   fire
that's not yet built.

                    World upon world!
                            World
under world!
            World waiting to be!

.

Then they light the fire.
They light the will.
They light the power to be.

.

Now Ekomina can say more of her Story:

*So the elder, the shaman, begins to climb. To the tree-
and snowline, to the rocks, and the one great rock in the
    rock-face.*

He leans his weight against it.
                                    It swings aside.
*A woman stands there. The wind whistles through her eyes.
"Old Woman! Grandfather killed the serpent!" She creeps
from rock to rock behind him as they go back down.
Grandfather, the Wolf Man, is waiting there.*

                                                          *

                                                   The elder
helps him pull the serpent out. The young one
still lies sleeping in its coils. He doesn't breathe.

Old Woman picks up a stone, a gleaming flint.
She splits the serpent's skull. She splits the serpent
down its spine. She pulls the young man's body out.
Cuts up the coils in packloads. They haul it all
back up the mountain.

．

If you look in her door you see
a sacred cave. It's a place for listening to the spirits.

There's a sweat lodge built on one side. The lodge of
Grandfather Wolf Man. And Old Woman.
                                    By now the elder
    knew
the two were spirits. Spirits that had the power.

They fire the sweat-lodge stones. They feed the stones
with water. The young man starts to breathe. His spirit
gleams behind his eyes.
                    Old Woman gives them
each a white flint knife.
                    Old Woman feeds them
out of white stone bowls that are thin as snowcrust.

.

"Now tell us why you're here," she says. "Tell us all!"

And he takes a breath and begins to tell them all.

THE LETTERS OF SILAS SOULE

October 7, 1863–August 29, 1864

In skating over thin ice,
our safety is in our speed.

R. W. EMERSON

October 7, 1863

Dearest Mother,

How proud you'd be to see
your eldest son! I'm acting adjutant general
for Colonel Chivington, inspection tours, reports,
the works! You and Sis both write that I should be
a Christian. Not be so wild. Well how
about a Methodist preacher for a boss? It's true,
my lips are innocent of rum and fine-cut chew,
I get along like I was seventeen
again. The colonel says I'll be a captain soon.
For now, no ostrich feathers in my cap. My brass
is getting green and my socks are wearing through.
The farther up in rank I go, the farther
off the payroll gets mislaid. Once
I wished to hie me hither, home, or California
or some other foreign place. I used to want
to pay my debts, but now this country's full
of ore and nuggets, half the miners talk
Chinese or Spanish, the debts are everywhere
along with IOUs for the pay we're owing.
All this to say I can't send any money
now, as much as I would like to. Yea,
blessed are the poor, for they have nothing to lose.
Or something like. Take heart, our last week's cloudburst

swept away the *Rocky Mountain News*,
or rather, all its fonts and plates and paper,
leaving the press to the hapless liars that own it.
Who can have the blues when the Creator moves
in such inscrutable and righteous ways?

Your loving,
Si

Christmas Eve, 1863
To: Mr. Walter Whitman, c/o Paymaster
Office, U.S. Army, Washington City

Dear Walt,

        Your book and letter both go everywhere
with me. And yes, the Army don't improve
a fellow much. A week ago, in Denver,
a cannibal from the South Sea islands whistled through a whalebone
   whalebone
in his lip and turned his joints all out of shape,
one-by-one and bone-by-bone. And all
for just a greenback dollar! You see how civilized
we are out here, when we put our wits to work!
Well that was last week. Now I'm just outside
Missouri City (Colorado) looking
for recruits. The end of the year is on us, the numbers
haven't shown, and any man with any
brains is back in Denver any way.
But we go on. The war is nothing here,
just bunting, flags, and flummadiddle. Of course,
they talk of Union, God, and Freedom. What keeps
the governor going is holy aurum. Gold.
My colonel is his bosom buddy, he says protected
and kept quiet Colorado yields up twenty
million cold in specie now and double
that in years to come. The national debt,

and so on. But in fact these gold fields all
sit squat in the middle of the Cheyenne lands, I mean
    squat,
by treaty, governor or no. The Cheyennes haven't
a clue to this. They just seem to dream, their dreams
are all of buffalo, and land, and spirits. And now,
of how to keep from starving. No holy light
of gold, no holy ghost to bring them food.
I hope they never get the clue! I've staked
out fifty claims, without a hope of working them.
Hope without work—isn't that the way
the poet put it? You must excuse my lack
of earnestness, nothing I say can satisfy
the sense of dread I feel in reading what you wrote
from Fredericksburg. That heap of amputated feet
ten yards outside the hospital "a full load
for a one horse cart," the medlies of wounds that range
from pretty bad to frightful, the sea of men
in tattered clothes, battered and bloody—and all
the while, you looking for your brother, only to find
    him . . .
I wish I knew where I could find my little
brother. I wish that I could even look for him,
but I can't. I look and look for a war that seems
to have fled my side of North America and come
to lie like an incubus on yours. You say you live
most frugally, you nurse the sick both North and South
alike. You say, at the last, "It is the worst of war."

Is there a better part? Boredom? Profiteering?
A second conquest (afterthought) of Indians?
I think of all I did in Kansas, then
I look at now, and wonder how "decease could call
me forth," as you put it. But I do believe you, Walt.
Yours is no book. I touched its poems and touched
the Quaker that you are. You won't get rich
as marshal of the bed pan and captain of the linen
    compress.
God bless you, Walt. If He is listening!

                                    Yours,
                                        Si

Denver City, Colorado Territory
August 29, 1864

Major Kit Carson
U.S. Scouts, New Mexico Territory

Dear Kit,

      Recall that pair of silver bars
we talked about so often? Well, the veil
of Mars's temple hath been rent in twain.
They're mine. But it took three years, including time
as adjutant and chief recruiting officer
for Colonel Chivington, two battles (distant, now),
and a ream of right-hand answers to dunnings from the
    left—
I mean, reports on operations no one
ever heard of, acknowledgments of food and gear
we never got, you know, the quartermasters.
I've been detailed to join the Regulars, to keep
the Injun hordes at bay. I doubt the destitute
Cheyennes could ever set these Methodists at hazard,
for sure no more than their own fire-eaters could!
I'm to Fort Lyon. That place is falling down,
not a spud to eat, the scurvy broken out.
THE PRIVILEGE OF RANK! I'll keep you posted.
Anyhow, the lodestone here in Denver
City still is gold. Alas, my days
with a placer pan are long since gone. The governor

is glad the Injuns too are gone, nothing to impede
the march of the quartz-mills, quote unquote. Except
the rains. Gullywashers, days of them. All
of Auraria washed away. The miners lost their tools
and tents, you never saw so many sober
angry men, for here. The rumor is,
the gov's about to raise another regiment
of Hundred Daysers. Three squares, a flop, and salvarsan.
But I'll be gone. I wouldn't want a regiment
like that within a hundred miles! Old Chiv's
been out of action since Apache Canyon.
Now he's running for a seat in Congress.
How can he run *and* take command? Don't answer.
I'll gladly take my leave of the colonel, I bequeath him
to some other adjutant. He ordered the Fords
"under special wartime powers" to buy a thousand
California broncos for the Daysers (ghosts
of the thousand mules and horses put to the sword
at Glorieta Pass?). Well, as they say, no matter,
scrip and greenbacks go flying through the air, the Rebs
have crossed Missouri into Kansas, the war's a mess.
Anyhow, the broncos: when the man-mountain colonel
gives his men the word to mount, his pick-and-shovel
dragoons will find they've fifty score unbroken,
skittish, wild-eyed cayuse! I can see it now.
Some stand on their heels, straight up in the air, and then
as suddenly pitch on their forelegs, sending the swearing
miners just like rockets off in space.

Some will stick their heads down, clump their feet
together, then hump their backsides like a camel,
with similar additions to the atmosphere. They roll,
they kick, hazes of malediction
rise like pillars of fire o'er Denver City!
They'll be a perfect study—jackrabbits for broncs,
jackasses for men. Prosit. You see, I'm now
a better soldier. And a worse subaltern.

                              Si

THE WOLVES OF HEAVEN

Northern Cheyenne Reservation, Montana
Morning, August 16, 1911

*In the sixth month, the white
snow is suddenly
seen to fly.
At the third watch, the disk of the
sun sends out
shining rays.
On the water blows the wind of
gentleness . . .
The land that is nowhere—that
is the true home.*

THE SECRET OF THE GOLDEN FLOWER

▼

It's the second dawn, and the beginning is aching to be
   born!

They're both awake, Ekomina and Frank Little Wolf,
and they're waiting for the light.
                              The rest of the people
are sleeping. You can hear the whiffling of horses
tethered beyond their lodges.
                              A baby cries.

Suddenly someone comes. Who? No one
can know. It's enough to know only that he is sent,
enough that he will help them start the spirit-work.

As first light breaks, he goes inside the Wolf Lodge.
He is the one who hollows out the fresh-scraped
earth, once with the thumb
                              and four times more
for the four horizons,
                              then raises up four mounds

with earth from the first,
                    then paints first two with madden-
    red
then two with crow-at-midnight,
                    then marks out wonderful
arms of light in white—the cross of daybreak
forming out of the One. And flowing outward,
everywhere!

．

Maheo is the One. Is at the center.
Is the one who speaks to Eagle. Who turns the feathers
of its head and neck the color of sun, for his hearing.

Listen, you! Listen to his deep voice singing!
Hang up bundles of sage! Bless what is coming
alive!

．

Ekomina can feel something stirring. What? Inside her something comes alive. A spirit-picture.

It's a plain as vast as this one, but farther on. Closer to Blue Mountain.

And a creek, with a grove of cottonwoods along its bend.

And her people. Pent-up. Hungry. They're there because they're made to be, and yet with quietness of spirit. One that whispers to them "More can come."

．

This was where
the massacre at Sandy Creek began? she asks herself.
She wants to know.

What does the smoke say?
She would know if she could smell the fires.

.

She thinks of the burial, two days ago. It was something
she'd set straight. One thing, one tiny thing,
now in its narrow house.

But she'll never know
just who it was. So many dead. Her grandmother,
Crow Woman. Hundreds more.

And what of those
who'd lived? Lived day by day to start the darkening
downward journey into shame for having been deceived.

Who'd trusted in the white man?
Black Kettle, for one.

It was he who said, "My shame is as big as the earth."
It was he who said it! The one who taught them!

.

She thinks: so many stories! Stories are the whole world!
The world we're in, the world that's yet to come,
they're all stories!

                    I want to know!
                                        I want to
tell them all!

             "Yes!" she hears the people
say.
        "Ekomina! Tell us all!"

THE LETTERS OF SILAS SOULE

October 9, 1864

*Adversity introduces a man
to himself.*

ANONYMOUS

Fort Lyon, Colorado Territory
October 9, 1864

Dear Sis,

       Three years in Denver City never
got me ready for this poor pathetic wickiup
of cavalry and Indians. The Army sent its troopers
into the wilderness, and closed its eyes.
I don't know who to blame—or who has suffered
more. The Indians, a few Arapaho
and thousands of Cheyennes, are all pent-up like snow
   geese
in October. They hear their fellows, they spread their
   wings,
us Blue Coats beat them down again. They're on
the dole, they dance, they only dream of hunting.
The Indian agent's wife sells pies she makes
with the Cheyenne flour allowance. Mrs. Colly
got more rations on her hands than the U.S. Cavalry
and Northern tribes combined. There's nothing to be done.
But I do ask, why such cruel neglect and misery?
And only us, the Cossacks, to give some consolation.
I'm serving with the Regulars. The generals, Blunt and
   Curtis,
want us local boys to chase the Indians.
They already tried their hand, at the end they shot
more buffalo than braves, and now they're off to chasing

86

Rebs (the other way—if they can find them!).
The fort command, Major Wynkoop, Major
Anthony and me, receive a stream of orders
out of Denver from the governor. They all add up
to "let 'em starve." Or "(impious expletive)
any man in sympathy with Indians!"
Or "lock them all away somewhere, forget them."
We do. But we lock ourselves away as well.
It started back on April 12 at a place
called Fremont's Orchard. The Cheyennes steal the stock
from an emigrant named Ripley. They also cut
the telegraph. This last is smart, but fatal.
Smart, because the Cheyennes know just where
the White Man's pulse is beating. Fatal, just
because the White Man knows they know it. One
reprisal follows on another, now
whole villages, warriors, women, children, even
dogs and horses massacred, put to the torch.
The Cheyennes also know a trick or two.
Some of them steal a girl named Laura Roper
out of Kansas, trade her from lodge to lodge,
then come up with her at our parley on the Smoky
Hill last month. A gift, they say. They want
to seal a peace "forever." Of course they'd killed
the father, the mother hanged herself, etc.
What do you do when you're standing on an anthill,
barefoot? You find a chief you think you trust,
then try to pair him with a chief of your own kind.

That was what we tried to do on the Smoky
Hill, to get their chiefs, Left Hand, Black Kettle,
with our Colonel Wynkoop, John Smith (a mountain man),
George Bent (a trader), yours truly. Even a chief
they call Bull Bear showed up. He heads an outfit
called "Dog Soldiers." Don't ask me why. Anyhow
we got a truce patched up between us. A war
with the Cheyennes now would only help the Rebs,
not us. Or that's the logic of it. Making it work
is more like putting shoes on a centipede.
The Cheyenne chiefs are full of honor for themselves,
none for their brothers-in-law just over the hill.
Our side swears eternal peace, but no one
knows what a testy Mormon teamster might
be prone to do to a red-face back-of-beyond
gentile. What we absolutely do not want
is another Hungate massacre, a family slaughtered
scalped and mutilated, bodies brought to Denver,
placed in a box and put on display so every
chucklehead can cry revenge. The Indian bodies
never get to town, and no one there
has ever laid their eyes on a plain of castaways
like this. Never. Out of sight and out
of mind. Or better yet, invisible and absolutely
gone. The governor got the tantrums over
what we did at the Smoky Hill, but finally
had to bend. He called a formal council
at Camp Weld to sign and seal a truce,

the Cheyenne chiefs all gussied up in beads
and feathers, our officers in brass and ostrich plumes,
interpreters and scribes and all solemnity.
White Antelope showed off a medal Millard Fillmore
gave him, Black Kettle said he made his peace
"with eyes shut, going with Blue Coats as if through fire."
My former boss, old Chiv, was full of bluff
and bluster, "All the soldiers in this country ride
at *my* command," and so on. When the governor signs,
he thinks to his own advantage of what the treaty
doesn't say. Another step in getting
all the gold fields, grazing lands, railroad
right of ways. The Indian doesn't sign,
he marks, he thinks of what he thinks the treaty
says. Protection. Rations. Peace. It says
what men say, now, and say again, and say
forever. The worst he can imagine? Shame. The Cheyenne
pledges all. Himself. That fact will sway
his fellows, even to end his life by his own
hand. The one in the middle of this congress of the deaf,
on our side, and mute, on theirs, is me. It takes
your spirits down an octave. It's every day,
you work at making bricks without the straw.
In the end, it's really like the Cheyennes see it—
we're worth about as much as we remember,
what we are is what we do. The rest
is dust. Which means I'm getting pretty dusty.
I get up dirty, eat some grits for breakfast,

ride through dust and sand, curry the burrs
out of my horse's coat, then lay my head
on a pillow tinged by the sandman's grubby hand.
I think I'll muster out. I dream of Maine
and marrying. Know of some rich widow? I'm something
of a catch. I've given up cigars, don't chew,
I've got a pile of IOUs for pay—
enough to start a bank! Write soon.

                                    Your loving,
                                        Si

3

THE ATTACK

November 29, 1864

*If men would learn from history,
what lessons it might teach us!
But passion and party blind our
eyes, and the light which
experience gives is a lantern on
the stern which shines only on
the waves behind us!*

S. T. COLERIDGE

▼

Monday after Thanksgiving. And the colonel has his
   regiment,
the Colorado Third. They're mounted Hundred-
Daysers, all volunteers, armed with rifles
muskets   carbines   Colts and Starrs   a hundred-
fifty-thousand cartridges twenty bags
of powder   a ton of lead   four howitzers   sabres
saddles   spurs   surcingles   all the quartermastering
anyone could want   and their guidons streaming in the
   wind.
But most of his troops are raw recruits. Come
close, you see only a scattering of uniforms,
you hear the slash of hooves through snowcrusts, the heaves
and rales from deep inside the horses' lungs.

The colonel looms in his saddle. At six feet four
he rides like an emperor next to his half-breed guide,
the talkative Robert Bent, who rattles on through the hours
toward daybreak, "Wolf, he howl. Injun dog
he hear that wolf, and he howl too. Injun
he hear dog. He lissen. He hear something,
then run off." The colonel laughs. He draws
his Colt and spins its cylinder in little clicks,
saying, "Jack, I haven't had an Indian
to eat for weeks. If you don't get your half-breed
ass in gear and lead us to that camp
I'll have it in a skillet for my breakfast."

Bent falls silent. Under the winter moon
the command moves like an amoeba over the landscape,
walk   trot   gallop   dismount and lead.
The colonel lets his troops take out their hardtack
for a gnaw. He hears a growl of discontent.
They can feel the bugs between their teeth but they can't
see them. The colonel chooses not to listen.
They slog on. Suddenly they're in a shallow lake.
Is the half-breed trying to sabotage the stores
of ammunition? The colonel orders strict precautions.
And he watches now a second line of columns
moving in behind them, the Regulars he seconded

at Fort Lyon. Their guide is Black Jim Beckwith,
they're detachments of the Colorado First, some
from Denver, some stationed at the fort. Volunteers.
And Regular Army. Beware of them, he thinks.
Some of them the day before had hunkered down,
refused to fight with Indians they said had saved
their lives. Typical of RA officers who fought
their best in finding reasons not to fight.
They'd even called the Cheyennes ill-treated,
   misunderstood,
prisoners already, camped along Sand Creek
at Army sufferance. "Not at my sufferance!"
the colonel roared, and he promptly wrapped his Third

in a rude embrace around Fort Lyon, posted
sentries, gave strict orders no one could leave.
He came down hard on all the officers, and one
especially, Captain Soule, who called his plan
of operations murder pure and simple.
The thought of it drives the colonel's fist into
his pommel. Damn all Indians, damn the murdering
Cheyennes, damn their massacres along the Platte,
damn Silas Soule, and damn all white men and officers
in sympathy with Indians. Let them get themselves out
of the service of these United States. His orders
come from the governor. He knows he can impose his will.

▼

Soule is in command of Company D,
Colorado First. He keeps them well apart
from the colonel's troops, if troops are what you call them—
Central City miners, flooded out
last summer, in for a hundred days of pay
then back to the diggings. Only a very few
with stomachs for a real campaign, and now with this cold
sick to death of soldiering. The kind of troops
no one can command, that early in this war to save
the Union proved the depths of their Dutch courage.
Ragtag volunteers that come sweeping down on Regulars
compelling them to do the dirty work

for Colonel Lunatic, for Chiv, as they call him,
whose evening entertainment starts when the cook
gets mad at someone, throws a burning brand
streaming like a comet, and soon the air is full
of brands, it's Farragut at New Orleans,
the night becomes a blaze of meteors
and shooting stars, and in the end there is no supper,
not even coffee, the volunteers get whooping
drunk while their colonel sits indoors, dressing
down the officers. This former circuit rider,
this Mason Methodist, size fourteen boots,
says he's come to bring them to a rendezvous. An apocalypse.

Dawn. Steel-gray as birdshot. They're riding on a sand hill
with the creek curving across the line of march
below. Only a gleam of water there,
cottonwoods and willows along the banks.
Clumps of lodges thrown down like pine cones catch
the sun's first rays. He counts a hundred fifteen,
eight Arapaho, the rest Cheyenne. Soule knows
the difference. He knows the colonel doesn't, doesn't
care, in fact—the Bloodless Third has come
for blood, for a victory in a year when nothing else
will do. They can't think any farther than their balls.
They're a brace of bulldogs straining at the leash

but it's the dogs below that give the first alarm—
a yip, a bark, a howl or two, then
duets, trios, soprano howls, tenor
yawps, a rising canon of mutts and mongrels
no one could sleep through. Except they do sleep through,
deep in a dream of trust because their Chief
Black Kettle smoked a peace pipe two months since
with Soule and the other officers, then saved the lives
of a hundred twenty troopers on the Smoky
Hill, and sleeps now with the Stars and Stripes
as keepsake by his pipe. The one who trusts the most
now sound asleep in the arms of his belief

as Soule counts off the seconds. Minutes. An Indian
woman steps from a lodge and gives a long
appraising look, then turns her head downstream
to where the Cheyennes keep their ponies tethered,
then back at them again. What does she think?
That they're a herd of buffalo, come from the Smoky Hill?
His heart is strangely moved by her delay.
It is as if the truth of what they are
must fight its way brain cell by brain cell while she gazes,
the promises, the treaties, peace pipes, blankets, gifts
thrust aside by a gleam of steel in morning
sunlight. She puts her head back, raises up her arms . . .

▼

He is asleep. He is talking to Coyote. Coyote is inside
Buffalo's skull. He has made himself small
to be the master of small spaces, to dance and sing
about himself, about his trickster ways.
He says "Come out, Coyote, come out I tell you."
Coyote keeps on dancing. "You're dancing on a pitfall."
Coyote laughs, "Oh no I'm not. Never
do I dance in a manscent. But you, Black Kettle,
where do you dance? This land in the hook of the curve
of Sandy Creek—isn't it a skull drawn
in sand? But where are its bones? The capsules of its eyes?
Whose scent do you dance and sing in, under the moon?"

He hears what Coyote says. He hears it heavily.
But he doesn't leave his sleep. Not yet. There is more
to ask of Coyote. He feels it. But what? He feels
it somewhere, but not upon his tongue. Somewhere
between his ears and eyes and mouth but not
upon his tongue. His enemy, slowness of speech.
That is why he waits to hear what Coyote says,
the master trickster always twenty paces
out ahead. Not the bravest, not
the best, but out ahead. As a young man, how
he wished to ride in front. And now like cottonwood
his wishes fill the winds with drifting feathers.

Coyote keeps on talking but his voice
is high and thin and fading. He can see that Coyote's
jaws are moving. That smile of his, that little
shake of his head in confidence. It makes him lean
down closer. There are tiny drummers, he can hear
them now, Coyote's kinsmen gathering in
from the flyways of geese and crane, from the runs
of prairie dog and rabbit. How can they squeeze
in such a space? And yet they seem to keep on
coming. A hubbub. He can hear the click
of bones as they bet their luck, he wants to cry out
and joke and boast with the best of Coyote's kin

but *eeeyaah* is what he hears, the little lighted
skull, the drummers, singers, dancers, gone.
A smell of ashes, buffalo robes, and dark.
Eeeyaah it comes again, he knows the voice
of Crow Woman, the rising note that stops in the back
of her throat, the warning note that brings him up
and running to the opening where he sees
her standing still as a blasted tree, her arms
extended at the ring of sand hills above the Creek.
There is a glint of light on steel, feathers
of breath from men and horses spinning upward,
a whinny, then a mule's complaint, then a shout

and the line of horsemen starts to spill over
the slope. He sounds Crow Woman's cry, then
again, and the camp has come alive with moving
men and women. He springs inside
his lodge, seizes his lance, the flag, and a white
linen rag. He ties the two of them to the shaft
and sweeps it back outside, raising it high
to the peak of his lodgepole where the wind unfurls them
    both.
The flag. Their very flag. And the flag of peace.
Together. He can see the columns riding toward them.
Mounted. Some are Blue Coats, their sabres drawn.
The high-pitched yells, the bugles. And now, the shooting.

▼

His orders. First, they strap their overcoats
to their saddles. Second, he sends three companies
between the lodges and the herds, then brings them to,
firing. *To open the ball* as the colonel likes
to put it, shouting then "I wouldn't tell you
men to kill the women and the children
but just remember all the women and the children
on the Platte these bloody savages have killed!"
Echoing the words the governor has used already
exterminate by any means   the phrase
filling the air, drumming like the hoofbeats
of the next three companies he orders into the bed

of Sandy Creek to add their fire. Then
the howitzers begin to belch while two more
companies scale the sand bluffs on the south
to catch the village in a cross fire. As he looks
down on the scene, the colonel notes with pleasure
and amusement how the bucks and squaws are running
first this way, then that, faster and faster
into a deadfall, showing signs of their slow-witted
surprise that white men could be masters of surprise.
I teach a lesson in bushwhacking no one forgets,
he thinks, savoring again his triumphs over
the Rebs at Apache Canyon, Glorieta Pass,

in '62 in a War to Save the Union
that since has walked around him, high and dry.
But those two battles had been wholly his, stamped
with his name and fame, first by turning down the gold
embroidered leaves of chaplain and taking up
a fighting rank, battalion major, then by the boldness
of his coup, routing a Rebel wagon train,
eighty-five bonfires of ammunition, clothing,
harness, forage, lighting up the night. Followed
by the solemn ritual of bayonetting more
than a thousand mules and horses on the spot,
three days of backbreaking butchery

before he sent his masterstroke, his brief
communiqué: *The West Is Saved, Colorado
Ours!* And what delirium had followed. And then
two years of silence. The growing buzz of rumors
that his bold success had been an overstatement.
Politics, jealousy . . . The savages are fleeing to the creek
    bed,
digging with their hands to scoop out holes to hide in.
He looks down now to count the units he's deployed
and comes up short by one. "It's Soule," the adjutant
reports, pointing to a company drifting slowly
out of range, "he's sitting on his hands,
he refused to give your orders to his men, he says

John Smith had got safe-conduct from the officers
into that camp two days ago. The mountain man.
Soule says he's pretty famous, he ain't a Indian,
and if your troopers kill him there'll be hell to pay."
Suddenly it's clear, the colonel's being outflanked
and it's Soule who's played this trick, Soule who mocks
    him,
smart-ass Silas Soule who boasts he almost
saved John Brown from hanging at Harper's Ferry.
The jolly jokester, as they call him, a veteran
as well of Apache Canyon, Glorieta Pass.
But well down somewhere in the ranks. Down where he'll
    soon be
again. And hurting. The colonel will see to that.

▼

He can tell the moment the adjutant relays his message.
Even from across a draw, Soule can see
the colonel freeze, then rise like a quill in his saddle.
Looking around. For him. Word of Smith
has changed nothing, not a thought for anything
except what's sitting on the colonel's shoulder whispering
murder in his ear. He can see a garrison flag
and a white flag flying from a lodgepole. Black Kettle
stands beneath, hands upraised and saying
something, the colonel's troops are closing slowly
firing on a whirling mass of men and women
howling dogs and huddled clumps of children

never in his life has he had to stand and watch
never had to say his no and stick by it
never worn a uniform that hangs like snakeskin
never knowingly deceived an officer
never seen such overwhelming force
never felt such heat of burning bloodlust
never wished the human race extinct
never known the hand of desperation at his throat
never felt his heart so fiercely quartered
never probed so near the nerve of hopelessness
never held the fiery coals of shame
never raised them to his lips and swallowed . . .

"Ain't this the shits." *It's his first lieutenant,*
Johnny Oster, just behind him. And farther
back, there's Hill, his sergeant. And Gibbons. Durkee.
Burns and Eaton. The privates, with him since '61.
Anderson and Burgess. Creech and Fairbanks.
Morris, Reading, Sherman. Vandenburgh.
Yarrow and Wilson. Suddenly it comes to him
he's not alone. Two score of them, four columns
wide, they're like blue adamant above
this wave of flotsam soldiery that surges over
the banks, firing on and on, firing
into the dead, killing the dead twice

over, some of them not waiting for the end
but taking out their bowie knives to start
to hack at the scalps, to take off fingers three
at a time and get at the rings, to take the noses,
take the ears, take the lips and testicles,
take the blankets, take the buffalo robes,
take the halters, take the knives and lances,
take the skirts and leggings, take the shirts
and moccasins, take the pipes, the bows
and arrows, take the beadwork, take the feathers,
take the sacred medicine, tomahawks, a pair
of rusty muskets, take the dolls and doll clothes,

it is as if there is no bottom. A cry goes up
and a Hundred Dayser gallops through the carnage
with a bloody pyramid of flesh hanging across
his saddle bow, the pubic hair and blood
glistening in the midday sun. They're cutting out
the private parts of squaws and next they'll throw
papooses in the air and stick them. And he just sits there.
He is beyond the reach of feeling when the colonel gallops
up and starts to yell at him. But Soule has died
already. Died to the life around him. Died
to threats and blustering. To the heat of bloodlust. And now
he knows the colonel plans to kill him, too.

▼

He calls out to his people not to give in to fear,
not to doubt the Blue Coats still protect them.
Words like his wishes, words like cottonwood.
White Antelope confronts him, tells him "Look
them in the eye, Black Kettle, see what kind of men
they are," then runs to the middle of the Creek, holding
his two arms high and naked in the air and calling
on the horsemen not to fire. He sees the riflemen
keep coming on, White Antelope now folds his arms,
he hears some snatches of his death song just before
the White Men shoot him down. He sees him fall.
The line wavers, knives begin to flash.

It is his shame. The bravest and the best of fighting chiefs
White Antelope has given up his spirit. With just
a cough. The smallest spiral of his breath. Gone.
Stifled by a tightening coil of White Men.
Some are Blue Coats, some are not. But not
a face familiar to him, he cannot tell a White Man
from a White Man, not a one who came for anything
but killing. And more than killing, more than merely
making dead. Desire, without the heat
of passion. Rage as cold as winter ice.
As the cold of snowbank sleep. From the land where men
no longer know themselves or know a brother.

His shame is as big as the earth. Black Kettle
has thought himself to be the only one who persevered
to be the friend of White Men. And now he sees
just where that trail has led him. He sees another
camp, another stream, at dawn, a time
not far ahead. Him, with his people. An attack
by Blue Coats. And one especially, whose blond and curling
scalplock falls from underneath his hat across
his neck and shoulders. The White Men cleaning out
the lodges, taking horses, taking fingers,
noses, ears. Everything. Time only
for a breath of death song, before the end.

He hears a whine, just a little whine
close to his ear. The voice of Coyote. "Black Kettle!"
he says, "Black Kettle, time to run and save
the people you can save!" He hears the voice
moving away from him and yet distinct
in all the din, "Come after me," it says
"come after me, I know a way out yet!
Follow the earth. Along the left-hand fork
of Sandy Creek. You wait too long, too long.
Now call who can be called, and follow me!"
He leaves his lodge to plunge into the scene around him,
shouting that they follow him, the men and women

hugging the ground, the thunder of the big guns
shaking the air, stopping their breath as they run
and stop, run and stop, threading their way
from burning lodge to bloating horse to creek bed
clumped with bodies. "Make yourself small!" He hears
the voice of Coyote, he says it to his followers, and he feels
a broken line behind him, a ragged trail
of stragglers coming now, still dodging, running
two lengths back and three lengths forward,
inching their way along the left-hand fork
where the White Men do not see them. Running hard,
their breath like telltale feathers in the emptiness of sky.

THE LETTERS OF SILAS SOULE

February 12, 1865–April 15, 1865

*The only joy in the world
is to begin.*

CESARE PAVESE

February 12, 1865
To: Mr. Walter Whitman, c/o Paymaster
Office, Washington City

Dear Walt,

The Cheyennes didn't get their lands.
Or food. Or justice. What they got was slaughtered.
Last November 29th. The governor sent out
Colonel Chivington and a regiment of Hundred Daysers
just to kill the ones that camped under our
protection down at Sandy Creek. Along
the way they managed to surround Fort Lyon, dragoon
the Colorado First and me. The colonel
cried for vengeance, said he'd string up any
son-of-a-bitch who'd bury their bodies or their bones,
quote unquote. It wasn't an army, it was
a mob. I flat refused to order in
my men or open fire. I soon found out
what's underneath that hide of Christian love.
That colonel-preacher went at me like I
was 666 itself. But I stuck fast.
Two days I testified before an Army board,
the colonel shouting challenges, the works. I thought
of you, and not without a smile. I mean,
here I am a soldier hectored by a colonel
just because I wouldn't fight. A preacher, who wanted
to kill the innocent, up against an infidel

who wouldn't. What do you make of that? Anyhow,
about a half the population want to kill me.
The other half are getting there. But some
Episcopals are showing signs of backbone and the Army's
on my side. Do I know what Quakers
must go through? Fraternal greetings.

Your friend,
Si

Dearest Mother,

           The news of Lincoln's death
just came. This last, most comfortless of losses!
We say to ourselves, it's just a month since he took
his oath, forswearing malice, pledging charity
for all. The great amendment passed, the slaves
are freed, a negro lawyer sworn before
the highest court, the bottom rails are now
on top. The Rebs gave up their flag at Appomattox
just five days ago, and today one shot
by one assassin ends it all. The victory
snatched away. What a nest of treachery this war
has grubbed up out from under rocks and hiding places
in men's souls. Devoured by dark desires they fight
to fight and kill to kill. Before I went
to Kansas I learned by heart that speech of his,
"The ballot is stronger than the bullet." Now I see,
bullets are strong! Our years in Kansas, all
my years out here, the constant grinding down
by death—how much is lost, never to be
retrieved! There's more. You heard from Sis about
the troubles with the Indians. Last November was a raid
by Hundred Daysers under Colonel Chivington
to kill Cheyennes at Sandy Creek. It was murder

pure and simple. You know your boy, no matter
how you push him, he's a bitter ender.
I wouldn't order in my men, the colonel
said he'd kill me for it. The whole affair
has gone before the Congress, the worthy Denverites
can't make up their mind if anyone's to blame
especially since the governor likes to run the colonel
neck and neck with Xerxes, Alexander,
Washington, and Grant. How can we let this country
run with the blood of settlers, quote unquote,
he wrapped the flag around him like a sheet of armor
plate, but out of the blue, spontaneous revulsion soon
set in. Enlistments dropped to nothing. Feelings
ran so high the generals did the unthinkable—
they named your son the Denver provost marshal!
It's a sign, they say, just how the Army really
feels about the colonel. And wouldn't my friend
the keeper of the Saint Joe jail have one big laugh
to see me now, the nemesis of horse thieves, the one
who puts the drunks and crooks away! You won't
believe that Colonel Chivington has mustered out.
I'd say he's shown his heels. He left the Army
flat, he's off to preaching to the frenzied, while I,
the one who swore all up and down I'd muster
out, I'm still in blue. Well Hail Columbia,
sometimes the truth of what you are is what
you don't discern until too late. And maybe
even then it's dim. But for me, it's bright,

brighter, brightest. For the last of my news is best
of all. Your son is a married man! Her name,
Theresa Coberly. Everyone calls her Hersa,
I call her everlasting love of my life.
Her family lives in Halfway House at Castle
Rock. She, her sister, and her mother are a fine
example of the virtues. Frank but modest, eyes
as clear as Rocky Mountain springs. The father
runs a stagecoach, whipsaws lumber, makes up
furniture for all the swells in Denver City.
I didn't know how gaining a crimson shoulder
knot might also open up the door to Dame
Matrimony, but there you are. I think the end
of the war brought up a whole new brace of angels
hale enough to turn old Jeremiah
into a jenny wren. In any case
your son transmogrified. He's the flower of the flock!
We even made it into Denver's best, who did
the honors yesterday forenoon with a present of the flaxen
order, immaculately white, one of those
Victoria pins connecting all four corners.
Also given, a specimen of the cunning art
of joinery, shape of a juvenile chair, so scooped
and sized to be of service with the former, shall we say
a year from now. All this was done by Episcopals
out of range of sensation preachers, village
doctors, and strong-minded women. I'm not a convert
yet but Hersa says I'm working up

the list. I can't explain my happiness. It came fast
and furious, alongside bitterness and threats. When
was it ever thus, that a soldier who wouldn't pull
a trigger wore such laurels?

Your loving,
Si

P. S. Laurels or no, she loves to dance!

THE WOLVES OF HEAVEN

Northern Cheyenne Reservation, Montana
Afternoon, August 16, 1911

*Love is space and time made
directly perceptible to the heart.*

MARCEL PROUST

▼

Now Ekomina says what comes next in her Story:

*The young man tells of the tall-grass country, of the game
that has gone into hiding. Of nothing to eat, and saving
the people.*

*Then Grandfather Wolf Man leaves the lodge.
When he comes back, he brings a young woman of a kind
they have never seen. She's good of all things in body.
She sings, and her hair on top is the color of the sun.*

*The elder knows she's the daughter of Earth and Thunder.
She has heard Maheo!*

.

Grandfather asks,
"Does one of you want to take this woman for your sister?

Or will one of you take this woman for your wife?"

*The elder is a shaman. He knows the spirits. He knows
the plenitude of things. He knows the oneness of the world
before the separation.*

*His is the road that leads him
back to the One. He can be painted red.
He can jump high over people. Can heal the sick.
He's been touched by the power of Thunder.*

He is Contrary.

Marriage is not his way.

.

He says, "My friend
is poorer than I am. He doesn't know the way
to the spirits yet.

Let him take her for his wife!

It will be the beginning of all that is to come!"

4

CLIPPING FROM THE
ROCKY MOUNTAIN NEWS

April 27, 1865

Who must die must die
in the dark, even though
he sells candles.

PROVERB

▼

Rites for Captain Silas Stillman Soule,
Provost Marshal

Despite the several attempts already made
on the life of Captain Soule, our provost marshal
took but few precautions Sunday night
as he and his charming helpmeet left the theatre.
When shots rang out he started toward the sounds
with wonted energy and courage; his wife was horrified
to hear another shot, and found her husband
lying in the street. A ball had entered through the captain's
cheek, thence upward into the brain. It killed
him instantly. The assassin dropped his pistol at the scene
and took to his heels in a trail of blood that led
in the direction of the military camps. Today in Saint
    Paul's
Church, Episcopal, the rites for one whom many
called their conscience gave those Denverites a chance
to show their sympathy. A veteran of Apache Canyon
who went on daring danger and disorder in our city's

streets, no fear of work, fatigue, or suffering
marked his character. He knew full well how many
threats were levied on his life. He did his duty
as he saw it. Not all have seen it his way,
but few have ever seen it more steadfastly.

The Governor's Speech

To strains of martial music played by the band
of the Colorado Third, our governor spoke at length
on the horror of the president's assassination, vowing
the traitor fiends who have devised this act will soon
be brought to reckoning! Cheers and unrestr . . .

AN INTERVIEW WITH COLONEL JOHN MILTON CHIVINGTON IN THE *DENVER INQUIRER*

November 30, 1868

*Nothing is enough for the man
for whom enough is too little.*

EPICURUS

▼

An Interview With Colonel John Milton Chivington!
Synopsis Of Sand Creek Investigations!! New Revelations!!
The Colonel's Appeal To The People Of Colorado!!!

—the first installment,
from our correspondent—

At home among his roses, the hero of Apache
Canyon bids us welcome. He's quick as a cat
and six feet four, with a voice still rich and weighty
with dispatch. How well he wears his nearly
fifty years, unburdened by the common cares!

"I stand forever by Sand Creek!" he testifies to us
as he did to Congress and to one and all in the four
eventful years gone by. Quickly he adds,
"A vast domain—gold and silver, timber,
grasslands, water—the patrimony of a people—this
is the legacy I leave America!"

As for controversy,
as for the Red Man?

"Lo, the poor Indian!
In his untutored greatness he has proved
himself the best of diplomats. Though not without
assistance of the high officials who plead his cause!
They would make of him the subject of a great
controversy. Many a villainous swindle
do they perpetrate, the 'friends' of his humanity!
Enough to put to blush the awful and unparalleled
commander of the sons of Sin, his Satanic
Majesty!"
We hear the colonel's voice
echo off the oak trees.

Followed by a heartfelt
laugh. "Now—would you know what people failed
to comprehend through all these years of inquisition?"

Many things—without a doubt!—is the germ
of our reply.

The colonel cuts us short:
"I mean, apart from the fact the Cheyennes fired
first! It's this—I'm one-eighth Indian!"

This revelation falls on us like a thunderstone!

"I never once denied it. Never was I asked!
People simply failed to want to know!"

He beckons us to sit. "My Indian blood—
I'm proud of it and always have been. My mother's
grandmother was a Mohawk. She named a son John
   Milton,
for the poet, and the name passed down to me. Not
Watchagottum or Gimmesumbo—as it could
so easily have been—but a name with a history, a name
to honor and respect! 'Never underestimate
the power in your name,' she said. 'If people can pronounce
   it,
if they know it, then they can know you too. If not,
you'll vanish in oblivion!' "

The watchword being candor,
Colonel Chivington continues: "I learned the lessons
of morality in sterner times. My father raised us
eighty miles from Cincinnati, deep
in a hardwood forest. I learned to hew
white oak and hickory into balk beams each exactly
eight feet long and smooth as if I'd planed them.
But my father—well, that was another story.
At age sixteen I learned to my eternal
shame just what my father was—a woods pirate!
He'd leave us in the morning, by evening he'd come back
with balks he'd snaked away from neighbors. Next year
I found him drinking to unconsciousness. In my hour of
    decision
I found but one alternative could lift me
out of darkness—the wondrous gospel preaching
and new life benediction of the church!

"And speaking of conversion, you should have been with us
at Sand Creek battlefield! The Cheyenne way
of fighting meant the squaws could wield their rifles
and their bowie knives with the same red-handed glee
as braves. I saw a hundred battlefield conversions
that day—I mean, when my troopers saw the truth,
they shot the ones who shot at them, braves
and squaws and all!"

His energy and our need for notes
require a pause. He unfolds an immaculate sudarium
and wipes his brow. As we dot an exclamation point
we ponder what our next inquiry should be.

                                        Surely
the charges made by John and Alma Lull
in the *Nebraska City News* must warrant a response.
(To those who failed to see their letter, the distracted
pair had written to protest the marriage of the colonel
to their daughter, Sarah, claiming she was but the recent
widow of the colonel's son—himself the issue
of the colonel's match with Martha Rollason,
but recently deceased—and, if we follow right,
implying impropriety for several years.)

He folds the linen, adjusts it in his pocket,
and makes deliberate reply: "I think it's best
you meet the lady. Old grudges sir, old grudges.
Two facts and seven fabrications make nine lies.
And I'm accused unjustly!" He deals a weary smile.

As if to prove him right, there is a rustle of silk
and crinoline. The youthful mistress of the colonel's house
appears! With a silvery laugh she bids us welcome
to her home, she who was chosen by the living namesake
of the bard who immortalized in verse that "nothing
lovelier can be found in woman than to study household
good, and good works in her husband to promote."

Then she ventures, "Sir, you see how my husband
suffers from his modesty. I'll put it right.
In the war, the governor named him to command because
his circuit riding took him everywhere, to every
niche and cover in the territory. Without authority
from Washington he raised a regiment himself!
And he didn't need a dollar. He issued drafts,
he mustered in two companies—and the rebels rued
the day he did, at Glorieta Pass."

"The only way to raise a force is raise
a force!" the colonel cries. "People have the right
to self-defense! The law is mostly a hindrance.
And yet, I did go down to Washington, I found
a way to crash the War Department gates,
I told them Lincoln gave us his permission
to raise the force already."

                          That was an invention, then?
we ask. He shrugs it off.

"What I said was, 'He said
"See my clerk there, lay the case before him.
Should Secretary Stanton turn you down, just come
to me and I will see that it is done."'

"It worked!
Oh, Stanton looked as though he'd bite my head off!
'Have you been up there bedeviling that poor soul
like everybody else?'

"I said, 'I never went
to Mister Lincoln, other than to pay respects
and shake his hand!'

"'Militias are a nuisance and a
rabble!'
Stanton cried.

—But in the end, he saw it my way!"

By stealth and guile! we have just begun to say
when Sarah cries, "Oh you can call it guile
but Colorado agonized—first, Civil War,
then an Indian War, deaths and massacres,
flour at fifty dollars gold a barrel!
Guile is guileless when it saves the innocent—"

"From worse than death!" the colonel interrupts. "I'd
    rather
be a private in a negro regiment than watch
the forces of rebellion raging in our streets!"

                                              The spectre
of the late hostilities, the pyramid of cruel deaths
that peaked in Father Abraham's assassination
all come up before our eyes. Amen
to that, we say. Nonetheless there are certain letters
going around, about Sand Creek.

                              "Are there!"
He laughs. "Really! They wouldn't be the first!"

Written by an officer, we say, a Regular. And we read
the text aloud, just as it came to hand:

"Four years ago, I had a funeral a day
for men who lost their lives by the most miserable
management ever known upon a battlefield.
A total of thirteen from one command, besides
some forty wounded. Any officer not
bent upon the rank of general or election to the Congress
could take a peaceable Indian camp with a couple
hundred men without ten casualties.
But I repeat, all Colonel Chivington
was working for was general's straps! The camp
was pacified already, no scalps were found, even
the weather lacked the drama the colonel claimed.
I didn't wear an overcoat and my bedding had been stolen!
As for spoils, the colonel had three quartermasters—
three!—not one of whom would tell me just how many
horses he went out with—or how many more
came back! My guess is, three hundred fifty more."

Silence. We wait to hear an answer, one
direct and apposite. Sarah is the one to break
the silence. "Grub!" The unexpected vocable is followed
by a catch of breath, as if her tongue is poised
to strike.

The colonel touches Sarah's hand
and says, "It was a scandal that while my troops
were fighting the Cheyennes some scoundrels shrunk
to plunder. But then, conceive of what we did.
We called ourselves the Colorado Indian Expedition.
We marched three hundred miles in ten days' time,
a hundred miles when snow was two feet deep.
The last night we did forty miles! At daylight
we attacked an entire Cheyenne camp, one hundred
thirty lodges, a thousand warriors strong—
plus squaws, don't forget the squaws! We killed
four chiefs, five hundred Indians, seized their stock
and lost nine killed and less than forty wounded.
We found a White Man's scalp not more than three days
    old.
In Denver, before we left, there had been a great
display of corpses scalped and mutilated by Cheyennes
so there was not a man among us who could think
the Cheyennes took that scalp in a friendly playful
manner! Or possibly those Indian saddle blankets
trimmed with scalps of White Women—with braids and
    fringes
of their hair—were just mementoes of the Cheyennes' great
affection for the whites! Unless we settled this
we'd not survive to statehood! Emigration at a halt,
eastern bankers holding off their money,
machinery to dig the mines just gathering rust—
we were being held as hostages by Stone Age savages

fraught with superstition and bully cruelty,
all dissemblers, none of them accountable,
who knew no law that anyone could understand!"

Time is slipping by, the question must be put:
How could someone one-eighth Indian fail
to sympathize with Indians? Our question might
be phrased with greater comity, but the onrush of his words
and our desire to know has only served
to sharpen up the discord of the facts.

                        It is the faithful
Sarah who now draws near us, her dainty eyelids
lowered, her graceful nostrils flared and waxen.
"Aha!" she cries, "the author's inclinations
have come out at last! You have no sense of decency!
You've come here just to trip us up!"

                        The colonel
takes her hand and says, "My dear, my dear,
keep in mind how agreeable it is, how comely,
how reviving to a soul so long afflicted by this curse
to know that God has given invincible might
to quell the wicked of the earth and give dominion
to the good, the wise, the just—the true believers!
Now, peace. I'll give the man his answer!"

He rises from his chair. He leans for emphasis, his gray
   eyes
cold as altar marble. "Surely, sir,
you cannot think so little of your God! This world
is delivered to our hand, sir, delivered for dominion!
Our Savior bids us make His excellence supreme!
And what an excellence it is—how indispensable to
   progress,
culture, commerce, mechanism! Think of it! You sit there,
writing. Readers await your words. The nation
reads, and when it acts, for our eternal good
there's righteousness like incense and piety like balm—our
   nation
under God, sir, under God! Oh the Indian
in war's a prodigy, in death a stoic, but he's dumb,
sir, dumb as a dog, he's ignorant of what can lift him!
What will save him? Offer him salvation! Offer
life! As he is, he'll never read a word
you're writing. I will! *I* am what conversion means!"

THE WOLVES OF HEAVEN

Northern Cheyenne Reservation, Montana
Morning, August 17, 1911

*To want to forget something
is to think of it.*

PROVERB

▼

Troubled sleep. She thought that she'd be free of it, but no.

To begin with, little dancing dreams. So small
you can hear them in the cooking pot. Can see their dust
rising out of a bowl of a pipe.

                    Too small for comfort.

Making her remember. The bundle. Down in its deep earth
    home.
She can feel. They laid it there, but it's not at rest.

.

There's a distant thrumming, somewhere. Echo
of an iron horse, chuffing its cinders at the stars?

The noise comes louder in her ears. And voices, reaching
across the air from somewhere.
                        Somewhere, but not
so far away. Praising and lamenting, on
and on.

       Prayers as free as the breath that says them.

.

They're singing, in a camp at the bend of a creek at the
    edge
of timber. A camp that will stay forever, staked
to the earth by memory.

                    It's the camp at Sandy Creek.
Why, why are they singing? What is there to sing about?

Once they were called the people. *Tsistsistas*.

                          Now they're
out
of the heat and cold forever.

▼

       Darkness. Is she awake?
Asleep?
       She can hear Black Kettle's words. They're clear
and bright as pebbles in a stream bed in the moonlight:

·

The white men make two wars. One to kill us.
And one to make sure no one will remember.

·

It's the war against memory that can never be redeemed.

·

White men, at Sandy Creek. They couldn't even
say their anger. None of them spoke our language,
none of us spoke theirs.

       What happened couldn't be spoken.

·

If there's no saying, there can be no vision,
no way of knowing, no where to follow.

·

                        A world without
  saying
can never have a story.

·

            No beginning,
no generation coming.
            Just killing off
the living,
        killing off the dying.

·

            Killing
to kill, without even the heat of wanting to.

·

Cold, cold is the war that kills off memory.

·

It keeps the ones who come from finding the words,
the first words, to start our story.

.

Starting the story
begins today!

Tsistsistas! *Remember, and resist!*

Ekomina knows
that she's been dreaming. When she wakes up, she'll go on
with her Story,
　　　　　the Story of the world, the world she's in
and the world that's yet to come!

She gives back her dream, and opens to her waking.

AN INTERVIEW WITH COLONEL JOHN MILTON CHIVINGTON IN THE *DENVER INQUIRER CONTINUED*

November 31, 1868

Chance does nothing that has
not been prepared beforehand.

ALEXIS DE TOCQUEVILLE

▼

An Interview With Colonel John Milton Chivington!
The Truth About His Saddle!!
More Revelations!!!

At home with the hero of Apache Canyon and his bride.
She takes his arm and smiles, exclaiming "John,
now is the time to show our friend your saddle!"

"The grandest gift a colonel ever had,"
he says, leading us under the oak trees to the house,
into the parlor, where the afternoon sun illuminates
a saddle-bridle set that stuns our senses—
the finest saddle leather, California
style, capped with solid *silver*, with our country's
coat of arms elaborately wrought
in native *gold*; a portrait of Washington, engraved
at cantle center, surmounted by a wreath of evergreens
in *gold*; a portrait of the colonel, surrounded by a
wreath of laurel, where flies our country's flag
in *silver* and *gold*; astride the saddletree,
a brace of holsters decked with pairs of crossed
sabres, in *gold*.

       The more we see, the more
we admire—the macheer, bound with gold-enameled
leather; the skirting corners, given to shields
with solid *silver* eagles at their centers, wings
extended, their breasts defended with shields of *gold*,
holding in their talons wreaths of solid *gold*.

The organs of our vision labor under such munificence!
Even the bridle is a treasure—the best black leather,
the brow-band bound and engraved with eagles bearing
the Stars and Stripes, full-spread, in *gold*; rosettes
at the ears and shields of stars and bars, in *gold*;
the check-straps, shields, and buckles *silver*, ornamented
with *gold* stars; a *silver* breast-plate, with a
second shield of Stars and Stripes in *gold*.

                                        We cannot
    speak—
"magnificent" would seem a sacrilege. Accouterments like
    these
were tribute to Spanish conquerors by Aztec kings!

"The gift of grateful friends," the colonel says.
"They know a man like me is never more
at home than in a saddle! You watch a lot of life
ride by up there—a lot of men who risk
their lives, cowards and renegades who don't or won't,
the aimless, the wiseacres, the burrs in your blanket—like
                                        what's-his-name,
Si Soule—all Dutch in the head and pigeon in his heart!
He's dead now, isn't he? Dark of the night, as I recall.
A coward cut down by a coward! If I know him,
he'll be leading a mutiny in hell by now!"

Of Soule we had not as yet inquired, but before
we can, Sarah says, "Even the great
John Smith caught hold of this saddle, begging the colonel
to save his skin!"

"The mountain man and trader!"
the colonel interjects. "I knew him at once!
We were sixty yards away, the Indians in full
combat, and I called out, 'Over here, Uncle John!
You'll be all right!' For an older man he could really
cut and run! I got him in between me
and my troops, then I hoisted him up here."

The colonel's
palm
rests on the pommel. "The Indians fled. 'Uncle
John, here you are risking life and limb,
making millions trading skins, and you're about
to lose your own!' I said. 'You mountain men
don't care for anything but profits!' And of course he had
those Cheyenne wives of his, and Heaven knows
how many half-breed cubs besides! Anyhow,
he didn't say a word, not no, not please,
not thank you. He just rode along, watching through half-
closed eyes at something none of us could see."

The deaths of Soule and the half-breed son of Smith
are much disputed, we remind him.

                              "Of Soule
I've said all I'm going to say! He wouldn't
take my orders, he wouldn't fire! The high
officials who love to plead the Indian cause
made sure that he would be protected!"

                              Not enough
to keep him alive, we venture. Or Smith. "Smith
was a different case," he says. "There's something about
a half-breed likely to excite repugnance, even
venom. Indian and white, each race embraces
only its own. A fact of nature, birds
and animals—"

              But how related to the case of young
Jack Smith? we interrupt. The facts are few but point
clearly to his execution by the colonel's troops.

"It depends which way you run, now doesn't it?"
the colonel says.

              Run? we ask.

                      "Yes, run!
You see your flag, you see your army, do you run
to greet it like a citizen? Or run off to join the savages?
I'd say which way you run will tell just what
you are!"

    But the boy would have looked around and seen
the slaughter of his dark-skinned brothers. How was the
    lad
supposed to know to save himself? And unlike
Soule, who was murdered in the middle of the night, young
    Jack
was taken to a lodge in the middle of the afternoon
and shot by a squad of soldiers, in earshot of his father.
The colonel had it in his power to save him. The colonel
might have made a very useful man of him.

"He was a man already," the colonel says.
"I don't think he would have served a useful purpose.
I had no orders to receive, and no advice to give.
Young Jack died accidentally, at an inspection of guns
carried out by soldiers under my command. That's all."

Sarah adds, "Your readers will do well to have
this side of things, you know!"

                        Which side?
we ask.

"Our side! Why just consider this.
There comes a young woman roughly clad, of striking
looks, with long red hair—oh, something prized
by savages! Her name: Lucinda Ewbanks, age
twenty-two, a baby at her breast. Born
in Pennsylvania, an emigrant to Kansas, she is one
of thousands of pilgrims heading west across
the plains in 1864—never
to arrive. She is overtaken by a party of Cheyennes!
First a Cheyenne chief named Two Face kills
her husband. When her baby cries and Two Face fails
to quiet it, he takes it by a foot and arm and dashes it
to the ground, jumping on its head and chest. He forces her
to dig its grave. No sooner done, he puts her
up for sale—three thousand pounds of flour,
sugar, coffee, and twenty steers for her,
the 'beautiful red head!' Instead, a gang of forty
savages descends on Two Face and carries her away!"

A moment's silence. "No need for all the details,
Sarah," the colonel says.

                    "Oh? Indeed!"
she says. "Just for once I wish the unconvinced
would listen! She cried: 'Never will I be the mother
of a child conceived in terror, ravished by a mob
of savages!'"

"Of course, I saw to it we got her back,"
the colonel adds. "The day my troops showed up
those Indians suddenly got the idea to repent!
We hanged Two Face in chains. In trace chains."

This last comes nearly in a whisper. The grisly particular
is barely out before Sarah adds, "Lucinda
Ewbanks later married a physician out
of gratitude for helping her avoid the fate
of motherhood that she had come so much to dread."

True, and touching, we reply, but a fact not suitable
for readers!

        "I warned you," she continues, "you and your
readers!
This is the other side! The truth!"

                                        "The point is,"
the colonel says, "you cannot fight for the end
of slavery in the South and wink at human chattel
on the plains! Poor Indians, indeed! They're completely
    shameless!
But no, you'll tell us next that uniforms hide all—
'Plate sin with gold and the sword of justice dulls!'
My Indian War was fought for selfish ends—
Colonel Chivington a candidate for Congress, for general's
straps, electioneering day and night!
Four years have passed and I succeed in one thing
only—in living a private life. If you
can call these interviews a private life!"

"There's nothing for it, but to show him," his Sarah
sighs. Walking to an antique chest, she opens
a drawer, takes out a folded piece of tissue,
and lays it in our lap. The paper holds a glossy
lock of auburn hair, and under it, a note:

"To Sarah, who never will forget my sufferings."
Signed, "Lucinda."

                             "I have companionship," she says,
"no matter what the change of fortune brings!"

With this, a tear has formed in the corner of her eye.
"What boots it at one gate to make defense, and at
another to let in the foe?" the colonel says,
and the conversation falters.

                    Sunlight is fading,
a sense of melancholy overcomes our intercourse.
One last inquiry yet remains, and we
must make it now. After the death of Soule,
Lieutenant Cannon, his replacement, swore out a warrant
for a man named Squiers for Soule's murder. He brought
    him
into custody. Two days later, Cannon
was dead of poisoning, Squiers had escaped. Was Squiers
a member of the colonel's regiment? Had the colonel
any knowledge of his whereabouts?

                    We hear
our questions dropping one by one in silence.
The colonel's eyelids droop, then close.

Evening shadows lengthen. After a moment
Sarah says, "It pains us much to say so
but Soule was something of a coward, a drunkard, and a
 thief.
He was in cahoots with traders like Uncle John
to profit from the Cheyennes. Who knows—to stir up war
against the whites, to close the gold fields, hold us
all for tribute! A man like him was capable
of anything!"

We direct our gaze at the colonel. His eyes
are open now. "So drunk he didn't know
his left hand from his right," he says. "And tell me what
should a field commander tolerate? He fought his best
in finding reasons not to fight. Remember
sir, the President's Committee on the Conduct of the War,
the Committees of the Congress, all of them took no action
for anything I did."

But had the colonel not resigned
and mustered out before the two committees
met? Was it not a fact that Colonel Chivington's
commission actually expired September 23rd
of 1864, two months before
Sand Creek? A technicality which placed the colonel well
outside the reach of military justice?

                              "I have nothing
more to say," he says, his eyelids closing.
We know the colonel's last official word
is spoken.

            By the way, we say, a dispatch has come
from Indian Territory south of Kansas.
The Seventh Cavalry attacked and burned a Cheyenne
camp and killed the chief, Black Kettle.

                                    "Seventh
Cavalry?" he asks, "I don't recall just who
commands them."

            A general, we reply. George Armstrong
    Custer.

"Golden-Scalp-Lock!" The colonel smiles. "An officer
you'll be hearing more about. The younger
generation takes the field. And Black Kettle dead.
How nice."

A tone of indifference, an inconclusive
handshake.
This is the subdued conclusion to our interview.
Turning to Sarah, we look upon a face more wan
and careworn than the one we beheld when we
arrived. There are lines around the eyes, the lips
no longer hold the curl of playfulness that made us
welcome. There is no doubt she loves the colonel—nay,
more than loves, she tends, glorifies, displays him
as the heraldry of all she worships in mankind.

And much there is to glorify. A man of little schooling,
without a day of military training, who traded in
the pulpit for the battlefield, for many he became
the counterpart of war itself.

                    A giant in stature,
a whirlwind in strife, he took his soldiers gladly
where the battles raged. The rebel forces vanquished,
he was honored by a grateful people. He could have lived
a circuit rider's life and preached to his dying
day were it not for the overwhelming cruelty
of Sand Creek.

Farewell, we say to Sarah. And farewell
to her colonel. For those of the martial disposition,
   Chivington
will ever be the very incarnation of war
and retribution. To Denver merchants Colonel Chivington
is Xerxes, Alexander, Caesar, all in one.
To cattlemen, the one who tipped the balance of the plains
from buffalo to beef. The name of their protector
to those who plumb the Rockies' depths for gold.

Yet doubts and shadows linger. That the Cheyenne camp
was peaceful was the finding of the Congress. The innocent
were slaughtered just because they were at hand.

We say this: the uniform of these United
States should ever be the emblem of humanity
and justice.
      The colonel broke the honor of that trust.
He planned and put in hand a massacre so foul
it would have set to shame the veriest "savage"
of all who were the victims of his cruelty.

The toll of the Indian Wars is not the count
of bodies only. It is invisible. It attacks the mind
and heart. It puts the soul to trial by asking,
"This nation under God? How shall it grow from roots
so deeply set in wrong?

                    And when it does,
its fruit—how can it prove a savor to our spirit?"

THE WOLVES OF HEAVEN

Northern Cheyenne Reservation, Montana
Afternoon, August 17, 1911

*If one is moved when not
stimulated by external things,
it is the movement of Heaven.*

THE SECRET OF THE GOLDEN FLOWER

▼

The people gather. "Day three is the marriage day!
Tell us all!" they tell her. "Tell us the beginning
of all that is yet to come!"

But it's not yet time.
Ekomina waits by the fire to start her Story.

·

One of the young women is painted with her father's paint.
Black suns, black moon. She takes the pipe and smokes it.

She's the daughter of Earth and Thunder.
                                        She's pledged to
    one
who'll be the Young Man, the one who found her.

                                        The
    daughter
of Earth and Thunder will marry him, for all of them.

·

He's hers. She's his.

　　　　She'll serve *Tsistsistas* now!

·

Now she's painted with her mother's paint. Green sun,
green moon.
New life is in her.

She's spring and rain and thunder!

·

Some of the people bring two wolfskins. One red,
one white. Red for the male, for day. White
for female and the night.

Wolves bring messages. They're
the ones who show how to coax the shy ones out
of hiding.

Then they bring a foxskin, for the light
of the morning star, whose rise is the call to hunt.

They paint the wolf- and foxskins. They fix four medicine
wheels to the hips and shoulders, and one to the middle
of each back.

For the white wolf, a strip of buffalo fur
behind her head. The tips of a pair of buffalo
horns behind her ears.

They're coming alive
in spirit! They're coming alive in their hands!

.

Now they'll hunt over earth like heaven!

·

Bring in food!
Scatter the corn! Feast on meat like the meat
of the serpent the Wolf Man killed!

Let it be meat
of the youngest of dogs. Not like the Wolf, yet like him.

Let it be meat from his Contrary, from his sacred Other!

Eat it, and there's food for the four horizons! Food
for the tree of the world!

And there'll be food for one and
all!

The sun's eye closes.

Ekomina's eyes are two weights
to carry.
She says, "Blow on the coals of the fire.
Blow on the coals of the heart. Keep them alive
for tomorrow!"

But the people cry, "Ekomina, the Story!"

So she says some more of her Story:

> The elder has said,
> "My friend is poorer than I am. He doesn't know
> the way to the spirits yet. Let him take
> this woman for a wife. It will be the beginning of all
> that is yet to come!"

> What the elder says, the younger
> one agrees to. So does Grandfather Wolf Man.

> Then he shows the three the four horizons.
> He shows them
> animals, so many animals!

> "Now, go to your home,"
> he says. "Go, and take our daughter with you.
> You, young man, are the luckiest one of all.
> Where she goes, everything I've shown you goes
> with her. That's her power—that every animal
> will come with her!"

．

He says to his daughter, "I send you out
for a very special reason. These people eat
only what they can snare. Just fish and songbirds.

Now that you'll be with them, they'll find what earth
can truly give them.

Show them the game, teach them
to think.

To hunt.

Teach them to stay warm in their skins."

．

"Listen to my words, *Tsistsistas*!" Ekomina says.

"Look at the game you've been given.
                              Look, and think!

Think of the hunt.
                    Think how you stay warm in your
   skins!"

·

It's night, and they sing songs of the wolf-spirits.

5

THE WOLVES OF HEAVEN

Northern Cheyenne Reservation, Montana
August 18, 1911

*To know the world you
must construct it.*

CESARE PAVESE

▼

Frank Little Wolf isn't happy. It's the fourth day, the day
when they don't eat at all.

Inside the camp,
around the Wolf Lodge, everyone must work.

They pitch
a second camp. Like their own, it faces
toward Blue Mountain.

But now the lodges are the lodges
of the animals,
of all the animals that Daughter has ever
brought them.

·

        Now every person in the camp, man
and woman,
        old and young,
            must find their way
to one of them.

        How do they do it?
           Masters are there
to show each one a way. Otters to the otter
lodge, cougars to the cougar,

           and everyone must come
to look and sound and be a creature of the Daughter!

.

Now the Contraries come, they set up their lodge.
And the keepers of the arrows, the sacred arrows that know
their way.

      And the wolfskins, Red and White: they're stuffed
with sacred grass,
              they're washed and limbered,
                        combed
and painted
        so the ones who put them on will feel
the power of the center,
            the center of the world.

                        The power
of the four horizons. Of every thing that goes on fours!

.

Who needs the story now?
                    Feel it!
Do it!

     This is the time to leave your name
behind,
          to change your self,
                         get rid of your old
heart.

     Shed your life's dead skin, leave it
in the sun!

·

      Ekomina laughs. All this is what they set
in motion,
       the two of them,
              the ones who pledged this
  Massaum.

But even so, Frank Little Wolf isn't happy.
Ekomina says it to him, Let it go!
Someone else can eat,
             someone else
can build a lodge,
          someone else can show
the ways of all the animals.
              Let it go!

He sits in the shade of the Wolf Lodge.
              He doesn't speak.

.

The lodges now are empty.
                    Dogs indoors.
Fires out.
            Everyone is watching. Waiting.

As they paint the ones who'll be the wolves, as they paint
the ones who are the Daughter and her husband,
                                                Ekomina
    says
some more of her Story:

．

Now they're warm in their skins,
and they say good-bye—Old Woman, Grandfather Wolf
* Man,*
Daughter, her Husband, and the Elder who's a shaman.

"Rest four times, my daughter," Grandfather says
"but travel straight to the Young Man's people!"

．

When the three reach camp they find they're followed
by families of otters,
                          by rafters of turkeys,
                                                by routes
of wolves,
          by buffalo in herds.

                          Animals fill
the horizon!
          Buffalo even rub their backs
against the Daughter's lodgepoles!

                                    They've come to offer
up themselves themselves.
                          How they love her!

Listen, you! This is the way Tsistsistas
won the right to hunt!

To receive the gift
of the lives of animals!

To be the people that we are
because whatever lives will come to us,

will offer up
itself as long as spirits talk with us!

As long
as Daughter does the bidding of the Old Ones.

·

But no one's perfect.

        *There's the day a buffalo calf
strays in, and Daughter's eye goes soft with pity.*

This is the thing that Grandfather won't hear of.
                                      Pity.

So Daughter must leave the camp.
                  *Back to the mountain
lodge, back to the Old Ones. To Grandfather
and Old Woman.*

          *And Young Man, her husband, follows too.
They go up the trail. They never came back again.*

．

Now, you see!

         What once was sure no longer is!

Once, the will was there.

         Now where's the way?

.

Find it.
      Find the way.

                For all fatigue,
and footsore,
      Tsistsistas
             find the spirit trail!

·

Frank Little Wolf gets up.

He leaves the shade of the Wolf
  Lodge.

He lights a pipe to bless the palings for a pound
that they must build.

It's a wide corral, with arms
as wide and open as a crescent moon in spring.
With cusps that will take in every animal of every
kind.

And they'll come home here,

each to its very own
lodge,
    at the center of the world.

．

Now everything is ready.
Only the oldest ones alive can give
the signal.

They're the ones to send off Red Wolf.
He runs out of camp to the calling song of the Wolf Master.

Then White Wolf runs out, too.

Now, you, listen!
Everything is still!

Down in her deep earth home,
Grandmother rules.

·

Ekomina leads them back to the Wolf Lodge one more time.

      Coals are glowing in the ashes of the fire. Sweet grass burns.

.

They sing calling-songs,
songs to the listening spirits.

And they answer!

THE OLD GENTLEMAN ON THE TRAIN

John Smith
June 8, 1871

*The tigers of wrath are wiser
than the horses of instruction.*

WILLIAM BLAKE

▼

"The heat is on, the goddamned heat is on!
Trust them to know or care!" A smell of hay
and coal smoke streams in the window and out a door
that wags half-open. Kansas is closing in
around him with a yawn, with busted sod and singsong
piety, with the click of wheels and bump of couplings
and rattling glass, on and on, State Line,
Edwardsville, Lenape, Stranger, L. and L.
Junction, bite after bite out of the pancake of the plains

and him in a moleskin coat, damask vest,
collar up to his Adam's apple, black string
tie and high black shoes. He looks more
like Marshall Field than a man who lived a lifetime
in the wilderness. But his feet are cold—how can his feet
be cold? A man who trapped and hunted all
the way from Westport to the Bitterroots, now his feet
are cold in these goddamned high black shoes! Deerskin,
now that was something else. Warm, limber . . .

Loose shoes, tight pussy, a warm place to take a shit.
Three things that take a man away from traps
and trading. One shot, one deer. Two shots, one deer.
Three shots, no deer. Chokecherries, and four around
a fire to eat them, stones and all, with a noise
like horses champing corn. Roasted fat-hump
ribs of buffalo, sliced boiled tongue, wild plums,
rose pods—the tastes and smells come thronging. For a
     moment
there's the sharp neat smell of smoke from cottonwood fires

and then he's back again, here on the Union
Pacific out of Westport to Fort Harker, a streamer
of smoke behind, smudging on the horizon. And farther
back, Washington, and the president of these United
     States,
America's Napoleon, where Smith has been interpreter
and shepherd for six Cheyenne and Arapaho chiefs
who sued for peace by begging "Give us something
to show for all our lands you've taken!" Followed
by lies and hedging and calls for studies and commissions

all so the theft of Indian lands can go on
as smooth as . . .

          "Mister, the heat ain't on, it's you!
Jest widen up yer window!" It's the brakeman
looking silly in his cap and badge. Puny
officials, wandering through the folds of his private life
like lice. Four times he's made this journey to the White
    House.
Three presidents, twenty years. At first, the Indians
got to talk chief talk. Now they simply
beg. No greenbacks in their pockets, no land for buffalo,

from Sand Creek the whites have even carted off
the bones of their Cheyenne victims. Sold them to some
    institute.
Young Jack's bones, for sure. Now they're jumbled
in some crate in Washington. The government gets
    it all . . .

He thinks of Jack, tall, light hair, gray eyes,
no way to tell him from a white man. His daddy's boy.
And yet he wasn't, he was Cheyenne, *Tsistsistas*,
with a youthful passion for his mother and her clan. The
    choice
of the son who would rebel against the father

and was then cut down by death.

                                Him.

                                        White Antelope.

Crow Woman.

                    Cheyennes by the hundreds.

                                        Si Soule in

    Denver,

Black Kettle and his people on the Washita.

                                        Yet somehow

Smith goes on, a wind-worn outcrop in a desert

of death. In Washington they call him "Indian lover."

The army calls him "squaw man." The mountain man

no longer gets respect, not since Sand Creek.

There's nothing now newcomers need to know.

Just kill off Indians, bust up the sod, dig gold.

And there's nowhere to go but forward . . .

                                        He nods. He

    can't

stay awake, he can't doze off. He'd like to, but his head

is lolling this way, that way. And now it's cold . . .

▼

He's setting traps along the Purgatoire. Lots
of beaver here. The others think the creek
was cleared, but he knows better. Or thinks he knows
till ten Arapahoes come screech-and-howling on to him
and there's nothing for it but to cache himself and let them
take his animals, tools, grub, and blanket roll.

What's left to eat is parfleche and a rawhide lariat,
and to drink, some Taos gutwarmer. He thinks, There's not
much choice—now you'll really have to stir
your stumps! He opens up the Taos and swizzles some,
then he hears a flute. A flute? Not
an Indian flute, but something with a wolfish turn to it.
He looks around. The buffalo grass is singed,
the rocks along the creekbed scorched and crusted
black. There are two big lizards there. No, two

somethings, standing straight, propped up by their tails
and dressed in Navajo-red, brass buttons, white
piping on their vests. And grinning.

                    "We've
expected you," one says.

                        "For years and years,"
the other says, and they bow.

                          He reaches for
his scalpknife but they go on grinning, saying
"Good morning, Sir! Shortcut to the mountains?" as if
standing at the entrance to some swank hotel. One
of them does a capriole and sings "Oh, do-dah, do!"
while the other claps his hands. Suddenly, Smith
is laughing.

                "Look! Look there!" they cry, and gambol
up beside him, pointing at the creekbank. It's an
   entrance—
there's a keystone arch, there's a light down under
shining up at them, and they're tugging at his sleeves and
   dancing
all around him crying "Shortcut!"

                              So he walks
inside and he hasn't gone two hundred yards
before he comes out in a canyon where he can run his hand
on rock walls smooth as beaverplew. The ground
is soft with cedar chips. And quiet. Overhead
the boughs of fir trees weave a soughing roof.
The light is going, but there are points still shining
out of tiny holes in the rock around him.

Then he meets a dead wall, solid black.
He jerks his head around and sees another
wall grown up behind him. That's it! he thinks,
this time you'll lose your hair for sure! and he's angry
yet not angry, certain that his time has come.

And with that, the darkness opens up. It's a room
as bright as day, and something like—he can't
quite decide just what it's like, but there's something—

"The company is waiting," he hears. His pockets suddenly
are emptied, his knife and purse and bottle gone.
They've picked me clean! he thinks, and hears a voice,
"Mister Smith, formerly a tailor's apprentice
of Lexington, Kentucky. A mountain man, and now
our visitor!" He hears the sounds of jollity
and there's a crowd of people all around him
saying, "Hush! Why, here's the mountain man!"

He feels his hair frizz out like a moulting buffalo.
"How do you do dear Mister Smith!" It's a grand
old gentleman in black, with bright gold spectacles,
and he's pulling out a notebook. "I've been watching you
    make
your way up there, and hoped that we might talk
down here." He claps his hands and the redcoat lizards
bring up chairs and a box of fat Havanas.

"Better than a pipe!" he finds himself saying as he reaches
out for one.

        "Take several, Mister Smith,"
the grand old gentleman insists, taking for himself.
Then he reaches out his finger to the end of Smith's
cigar and touches it. The smoke springs up as if
he'd torched it with a living coal and Smith can feel
his feet go cold.

        He says, "The devil!"

                  "The same!"
the grand old gentleman replies, taking up a comb
of pearl and tortoise shell to dress his beard.

"How—?" Smith begins to ask, but the old gentleman
   laughs.

"Evil communications corrupt good manners, sir!"

"You mean, you really are—?" Smith asks.

                  "Of course!"
The old gentleman combs his beard. Now Smith feels
he's known this man, but where? He feels his hands
rise up to offer his cigar to sky and earth
Tsistsistas-style.

        "Now that's not very nice," the old
gentleman objects. He's staring at the cigar. "Smith,
I beg you! Out upon such superstitions!

"We cut a Christian figure here. It's a tribute
of sorts, don't you see?" Smith doesn't see
and he wants his knife back. "No use in that, sir,"
the old gentleman continues. "And alas for your old habits.
You cannot kill the dead! Ah, I see your equilibrium
has been destroyed. Believe me I did not intend it!
Come. Open up that door for us." He gestures
at a bright brass doorknob Smith just now has noticed.
Oh no, Smith thinks, you won't get me that way!

Then he remembers, there's nowhere to go but forward
so he grasps and turns and a door swings open noiselessly.
"Good hinges," Smith blurts out, and brings a smile to the
     grand
old gentleman, who says "Oh we have the raw materials
and time!" as they step into a great salon—high ceiling,
chandeliers, portraits on the walls, carpets underfoot,
table in the middle, a bottle, a pair of glasses.
Smith is sure he's been here, a familiar feeling
has him by the neck but his tongue keeps hanging loose.

"Just call me Brother Bender," says the grand old
     gentleman.
He pours two glasses. Smith asks, "Did you say
Brother Bender? Don't tell me you're a preacher!
One of the hallelujah boys with eyeballs
white as a mule on a mountain trail in winter?"

Brother Bender laughs. "I could have been.
Here's to you!" Smith empties his glass. The taste
is nothing like the Taos—it's warm and smooth, and he
    feels
a need for talking taking hold of his tongue.

Brother Bender says, "Oh yes, I could
have been the kind that does up two long sermons
of a Sunday, then plays nickel-ante poker
with the deacons all night long for the takings bagged
and counted. And when he gets in debt, makes meat of his
    congregation
for all the poor heathens out in Timbuctoo
dying for want of a gospel preacher, condemned
to eternal hell because they'll only part with noisy
dimes and nickels, not the silent grace
of greenbacks."

Smith says, "I ain't been overly good
since I came to the mountains. Don't look to me for pity.
That's just the way the stick floats."

"Of course!" replies
his host. "The world is—why, it's just the world.
Yet it's given for our dominion! Can you imagine—
giving a world that's dark for half the time
and twilight half the other half? Some gift!
How can you rule what you can't even see?"

The question
tickles Smith. He's never thought of it like that.

It reminds him of Si Soule. "I've been in on every Indian
treaty on the plains. Translator, English to Cheyenne
and back again. Speaker to the House of the deaf
on one side, and the mute, on the other."

Brother Bender
laughs. "You're a man of spirit!" he cries.

"Spirit?"
Smith asks. And then strangely, he feels his heart begin
to break. Why should it go to pieces while his host
is laughing?

It's the image in his mind again. The end
of the road of the treaties and palaver and pipes and gifts:

the massacre at Sand Creek, the mob of Hundred Daysers
milling around his son, calling him son-of-a-bitch
that should have been shot long since. And Jack,
with his gray eyes cold with hate and anger, shouting
that he didn't give a damn. If they wanted so bad
to kill him, shoot him! And the Hundred Daysers raging
how they'd kill his father and anybody else
that loved the Indians, when Colonel Chivington had called
"Come out, Uncle John! Come on out of there!"

Jack's eyes had turned on him and staked him to the spot.
Never before, never since, has Smith
had someone stare directly through his flesh
into the passageways where his deepest feelings nest.
In that instant Smith had seen a cave inside
himself, a cave whose walls were covered with delicate
meticulous inscrutable tracings. No one, not Jack,
not he, would ever know their meaning. What he knew
was what he'd heard. The colonel's voice, as cold as stone.

He'd turned away and gone outside. A pistol
shot rang out, and Jack was dead. But not
dead enough. That was when the whoops and yells
began, and a Hundred Dayser got his mount,
tied Jack's feet together, and dragged him out
of camp and back and forth across the prairie.
Others rode to join him, whooping, yelling,
and for what? Who was the hero, what had been
the prize? The deaf exulted, the mute were dead.

"What I meant was this—you know too much!"
says Brother Bender. "That's why I've had my eye
on you," pouring him another drink.
But Smith is raking up the coals of his feelings
yet, he doesn't believe, not in Brother
Bender, not in chitchat, not in anything
but his vision of those tracings deep inside. He'll carry it
to his grave. Knowing it was he who turned his back
on his own boy. He alone, and no one else.

And here's the place it's taken him, Hell, and a go-round
with its master, who might as well have been the president's
private secretary.
                    Was, in fact, a double
for the man! *That* is what Smith has been groping for—
the model of that master flatterer, magician of contracts
and procurements, maker of sutlers and Indian agents—
Midas, king of the government dirt that he can turn
to gold!
                    That seen, now Smith begins to see
familiar whiskers in these portraits on the walls. It's a
    gallery
of sharp-set rogues, Republicans and Democrats, ready
to peel the Indian off the surface of the earth.
                                            "No more,"
Smith says, pushing his glass away, "and thank you
for your kindness. It's time I broke for timber. Which way
to the mountains?"
                    "Why sir, you've had a change of
    heart?"
the other asks. "May I know why? Was there something
lacking in my course of conduct? Come, sir, never
fear to speak your mind."
                    "I spoke my mind,"
Smith says, "I spoke it six ways round and then some."

"Out-of-the-way life. Casehardened habits. A pity.
I can tell you're well-disposed to higher things.
Not long ago the court of a reigning king
was horrified by an envoy of your president who dealt out
    cards
while licking thumb-and-finger, thumb-and-finger—
but for that, he might have been thought a merchant
    prince!"

Smith turns away. His heart is now too heavy
for this talk he's heard before. In the White House. "I'm
    off,"
he says, turning to find the door and go.

Brother Bender says, "I'll see you out."
His tone is all regret and beg-your-pardon.
This time, when they go out through the noiseless door
    they're in
a corridor, or is it a cave, Smith can't tell which.
It's dark. Doors are slamming. There are shouts, and
    clangs
of iron on iron. It's damp. Brother Bender
holds a candle. Grease is running down
its block. Its blaze clings to the wick as if it hates
to leave it, then gives itself to smoke as if in mourning.

It's cold again. Smith can hear the echo
of their footsteps, and a chill begins to take him. He needs
a drink. He needs it bad. Just then the flame
flares up and he's blinded by the light. He rubs his eyes
and sees a spotted python coming at him with its red-
and-yellow eyes and thin white fangs and a tongue
that's sharp and quick as a panther's paw. Fire blazes
out of niches in the walls. The lizards have come back
with willow lances, they thrust them at his legs and ankles

and Smith begins to hear a wispy hiss
coming from them, drawn out and given breath
until he hears it "Smith!—Smith!—"

                                  Now he's straining
every joint and muscle, and fear has put
the taste of gunmetal in his mouth. Shrieks have started up
behind him—it's as if the whole *caballada* of Hell
has broken loose.

                    The stench of burning sulfur
stings his lungs. This place is not quite full,
Smith thinks. Not quite, and I'm the hottest on their list!

He turns his head. The face of Brother Bender
hangs there, next to his. Serene. Gray eyes
staring into his. Smith hadn't seen, but yes,
they're gray. And cold. They're Jack's. He can feel the heat
from the fires behind him, they're at his shoulders now
and something's reaching out, it comes around
his arms—it's the python, its coils are winding one
upon another, Smith can see the spots
flexing closer to his eyes, blurring into whorls

and mazy patterns and suddenly they're a wall, a coiling
living wall, covered with delicate meticulous
inscrutable tracings, there, before his eyes,
he's falling into himself, into warmth
and into blackness with a long and wolfish yell
ringing in his ears and a burning smell and thirst
as his feet begin to fail him, begin to drag him
downward into darkness, into a seething formless
magma that is no river, no way to anywhere but . . .

▼

. . . He's awake. It's not the Purgatoire he's on, he's on
the train from Westport to Fort Harker. The window's
    hanging
open, he's sweating in his socks, he's looking into the eyes
of a brakeman chanting "You all right?" and Smith
must raise his aching head to nod an answer.
The brakeman gives a loud opinion, "Yer sick,
old scout! Close her up," and bangs the window
shut. Smith can feel the prickle of the eyes
around him. Shit, I cried out in my sleep, he thinks
and holds his head up, eyes straight ahead. Indifferent.
Resolute. Nowhere to go but forward.

                              And the train
keeps plunging on, click after clack, switch
after siding, cattle pen and telegraph pole,
one upon another, the tracks like iron arteries
pumping people, wagons, horses, guns,
priests and politicians, gazettes and gamblers
into the waiting body of the land that he once
tracked and trapped in, innocent as an angel

and free as an eagle, owned only by the airs
that bore him, nothing else. Nothing else . . .

Smith wipes his face. He knows he's sick with fever,
all he wants to do is get there, Darlington
Agency, where his Cheyenne wife is waiting.
Get into his blankets, go to sleep by the fire . . .

After Washington, they'd hauled the delegation up
to New York City. Took them to the port, where ships
nosed in from Bremerhaven, Bristol, Bergen,

where lines of immigrants came snaking through the
    Customs,
where there were heaps of trunks and wailing kids and
    railroad
cars backed up to take them on, smoke hanging
everywhere, the coughing of the engines like the beating of
    a heart
that pushed it on, all of it, ship after ship, line
after line, train after train. The president's man
had said, "You see these white men coming from the sea?
They come and come! The sea has ships without number,
these men must find new homes. They need the land!"

At first the chiefs had watched in terror. Then
it slowly dawned on them just what that mighty
ocean brought ashore. And would bring ashore
like this forever. Smith could see the muscles
in their necks begin to slacken, their eyes grow dull.
They had just walked off the edge of their world and found
another that was juggernaut to everything they loved and
    hoped.

It came from the sea, from a place not one of them had
    dreamed of.
In a moment the plains had disappeared, the buffalo,

the life that was as close to them as skin . . .

Smith's skin
is burning. There's a force at work in his life too,
one he's never had his way with.

Oh my son!
The words come at him, cut him like the python's fangs
and he feels there's something going out of him like blood
and he can't stop it . . .

Smith settles in his seat, closes
his eyes. And then he sees again those riddle
tracings.

Now he's opening up the volume of a life
he's never lived, written in some language where the letters
look exactly like those tracings. If he could only . . .

THE WOLVES OF HEAVEN

Northern Cheyenne Reservation, Montana
August 19, 1911

*Man does not possess freedom
as a property;
it is the contrary that is true.*

MARTIN HEIDEGGER

▼

The last day, the best of all.

                          They're up with the morning
star. With the spirits,
                    with the fox who is graceful and
  intricate.

And the people, all of them dressed in skins.
                          They've
  become
the animals!

.

You hear so many flutes!
                    You smell the
   sweetness
of sage!

        The medicine lance appears!
                          Such
running and prayers and shouting!

·

It's Ekomina who puts
on
a wolfskin now:
she stands at a cusp of the crescent.

She's the one who calls the animals in.
Listen, you. To hunt truly is to call the animals,
not to chase them!
Just see what her call can do:

Buffalo. Elk. Antelope. Deer. Otter.
Wolf. Turkey and Crane.
                    Badger, Coyote,
Grizzly Bear, Cougar, Black Bear, Eagle—
they come jumping and dancing and running,
come into the arms of the crescent, spitting and crying
and creeping and whining!
                    They keep on coming and
    coming!

·

The Contraries burst from their lodge with sky-bows and
    arrows!

They're not like hunters, yet like them.
                                             They know the
    spirits.

They are our Others!

·

Animals are staggering. Falling.
They bleed and they bellow when they try to get up again.

Bring up the sick, bring up the ones who need blessings!
Heal with this power!

·

Four times they run this hunt.

They run it past the Red Wolf lodge
                                right
in the heart of the Blue Sky lodge
                                in the presence of the
    Four
in sight of the Seven
                    in the power that's given by Maheo!

．

At last, all of them stand in the great enclosure.
Not one will go back to a lodge.

> The sacred pipe,
the medicine lance, the buffalo skull—

> Ekomina
holds them up, to show their power!

．

All of a sudden Coyote comes!
                          He runs,
he feints, he dodges around.
                          He shows how well
his wiles can serve the sacred wolf, his master.

Then Fox leaps up.
                   He grabs the meat from the medicine
lance!

    Contraries catch him, snatch it back
and throw out bits and pieces to the people.

·

Coyote cuts loose again! He leads them all
out of the great corral,

out of the crescent
moon
and down toward water.

On the way they stop
four times. All of them sing the Massaum song.

,

.

You, race to the river!
                    Fill your mouth
with water!
            Wash!
                    Give water to a woman!
                                    Laugh!

Brush the dust away from your eyes with sage!

·

Ekomina, Frank Little Wolf, and the oldest one alive,
they're in the Wolf Lodge now.

They're smoking
the sacred pipe.

Wherever ashes fall, they fall
on *Tsistsistas* ground.

·

The ashes are brushed away.
The sand paintings, they're brushed away as well.

The pipe,
the feathers, skins, and rattles have to go.

.

Only the tree and lodgepoles stay.

                              They can be
a home for spirits, now.
                    They can rest.

Listen, there's a sound of wind somewhere.

You hear?
        It's whistling through someone's eyes.

                                It says:
we're camped in short-grass country, and it's ours.